"What is the right adjective for Lorenzo Albacete's generosity of spirit, daringness of intellect, breadth of learning, and largeness of heart? Could it be. . .catholic?"

—HENDRIK HERTZBERG
Senior editor and staff writer at *The New Yorker*

"I once said that Lorenzo Albacete's journey was like the road to Emmaus: where Christ the stranger becomes Christ the friend and liberator. *The Relevance of the Stars* makes the map of that itinerary available to all of us. Among other things, it shows us how to avoid the dead ends of modernity—especially dualism and moralism—and points the way toward what we most desire: to know oneself loved by the one who walks beside us. This powerful book speaks equally to mind and heart."

—SEÁN CARDINAL O'MALLEY
Archbishop of Boston

"The golden thread that unites all of these remarkable essays is Albacete's pursuit of the ultimate question: What is the religious sense? For him, it is not to be found in an idea or in a dogma, but in an encounter with a person. The religious sense is rooted in our thirst for beauty, for truth, and for justice. It is experienced by all of us in our desire for More."

—HELEN WHITNEY
Producer/Director of documentaries for PBS

"St. John Paul II told us of the need for an evangelization new, not in its message, but in its "ardor, methods, and expression." No one understood this better than the late Monsignor Lorenzo Albacete. The essays presented here are brilliant, insightful, and inspiring examples from a life changed in the mystery of the encounter with Jesus Christ and communicated by one of the most unique Christian thinkers of our time. Here is the remarkable testimonial of a remarkable Christian from which we all may benefit."

—CARL A. ANDERSON
Supreme Knight of the Knights of Columbus

"Here, in this book by the only physicist I know who was also a monsignor, is the balm we all need to help us handle our fears and our anger in these difficult days. Lorenzo Albacete's unique capacity to bring love and caring to the front of any topic shines forth—his readers will quickly recognize how much they needed to hear this voice."

—ROBERT POLLACK
Professor of Biological Sciences, Columbia University

"This is a provocative book, incarnated in reality. Albacete demonstrates an extraordinary depth of judgment concerning American history. His understanding of the meaning of personhood and community carries conviction because it is always grounded in his own experience."

—ANGELO CARDINAL SCOLA
Archbishop Emeritus of Milan

"Monsignor Lorenzo Albacete had a tremendous impact on my life. Once at a religious rally in New York City, two people approached and inquired, 'Is this a protest?' Albacete exuberantly replied, 'Yes!' They asked, 'What are you protesting?' Monsignor responded, 'Dualism!' As the people hurried to get away, Albacete shouted after them, 'Don't go! The dualists will get you!' It is just such inimitable wisdom, faith, genius, and humor that fills this beautiful, indispensable book."

—FR. PETER JOHN CAMERON, O.P.
Founding editor-in-chief of *Magnificat*

THE RELEVANCE OF THE STARS

The Relevance of the Stars

Christ, Culture, Destiny

LORENZO ALBACETE

Edited by
LISA LICKONA
& GREGORY WOLFE

 SLANT

Slant
An Imprint of Wipf and Stock Publishers
199 W. 8th Ave., Suite 3
Eugene, OR 97401

www.slantbooks.com

HARDCOVER ISBN: 978-1-7252-7385-6
PAPERBACK ISBN: 978-1-7252-7384-9
EBOOK ISBN: 978-1-7252-7386-3

Cataloguing-in-Publication data:

Names: Albacete, Lorenzo.

Title: The relevance of the stars: Christ, culture, destiny. / Lorenzo Albacete.

Description: Eugene, OR: Slant, 2021.

Identifiers: ISBN 978-1-7252-7385-6 (hardcover) |ISBN 978-1-7252-7384-9 (paperback) | ISBN 978-1-7252-7386-3 (ebook)

Subjects: LCSH: Christianity and culture | Christianity and culture — United States. | Christianity — United States — 21st century. | Christian life — Catholic authors.

Classification: BX2350.3.A44 2021 (paperback) | BX2350.3 A44 (ebook)

01/12/21

Contents

Introduction

THE LATE MONSIGNOR Lorenzo Albacete was one of those people for whom the phrase "larger than life" seems to have been coined. Like Walt Whitman, he contained multitudes. Albacete had an outsized personality, an outsized intellect, and—as those lucky enough to know him intimately were well aware—an outsized heart. The temptation for those who loved and admired him—as the editors of this volume did and do—is to saddle a book like this with the sort of outsized apparatus—a long introduction, footnotes, index, the works—often used to honor a great person.

That temptation is even greater in the current instance because *The Relevance of the Stars* is the first attempt to gather in one place Albacete's most substantial essays and addresses, the work that reflects the full scope of his theological and cultural wisdom.

But this is a temptation we have chosen to resist. Lorenzo Albacete was a brilliant theologian and a famously witty raconteur about whom there are many classic anecdotes begging to be told, but he was above all a great communicator—and his lucid and provocative prose deserves the fastest and most direct route into the minds and hearts of you, his readers.

Our task in this introduction, therefore, is simply to offer some context for the material collected in these pages.

Lorenzo Manuel Albacete Cintrón was born in 1941 in San Juan, Puerto Rico. As a young man, he came to Washington, DC, to attend college for aeronautical engineering and to pursue graduate work in aerospace physics. After working as a research scientist for seven years at the Naval Ordnance Laboratory, he responded to a call to the priesthood in the Washington archdiocese.

Albacete's brilliance as a theologian was recognized early on and sought after by those in the hierarchy of the Roman Catholic Church. It was while Albacete was serving as an advisor to Cardinal William Baum that he first met the then Archbishop of Kraków, Karol Wojtyla, and the two became friends. When Albacete went to Rome for graduate theological studies a few years later, he focused his work on the thought of Wojtyla, who by that time had been elected Pope John Paul II. In 1983, Albacete attained his doctorate in Sacred Theology with a dissertation on the pope's theological anthropology.

After his return to the U.S., he helped to found the Washington, DC, campus of the Pope John Paul II Institute for Studies on Marriage and Family, a graduate school of theology, where he taught for ten years. From 1997 to 1998 he served as President of the Pontifical University of Puerto Rico. The following year he was appointed visiting professor at St. Joseph's Seminary in New York.

Shortly after Albacete moved to New York in 1998, he was asked to a dinner where he met a handful of people influential in New York's mainstream media. The friendships that arose in this circle led to Albacete's cover story for *The New Yorker* on Pope John Paul II's visit to Cuba, columns for *The New York Times*, appearances on The Charlie Rose Show and CNN, a surprisingly friendly public debate with noted atheist Christopher Hitchens, and a continuing relationship with the PBS series *Frontline* as a commentator and advisor.

Yet even as these friendships blossomed and exciting opportunities emerged, it was another, earlier encounter that was to have the greatest influence on Albacete's life: a meeting in the early 1990s with an Italian priest from Milan named Luigi Giussani (1922–2005). Monsignor Giussani was the founder of the ecclesial movement Communion and Liberation (CL), which traced its origins back to his experience teaching high school students in the 1950s.

Since his early days as a scientist, Albacete had grappled with a question that became a lifelong preoccupation: the relation between faith and life. To his colleagues, Albacete was an anomaly: a man who lived with a clear passion for scientific research while at the same time clinging to an ancient and seemingly irrelevant creed. His desire not only to respond to others but to more fully understand his own path led Albacete first to the work of the Second Vatican Council and then, in his theological studies, to John Paul II's thought.

It was in the pontiff's "Christocentrism" that Albacete found a satisfactory explanation of his own experience of the integration of faith and life: insofar as all things are created in Christ, no worldly realities lie outside him. And insofar as Christ is man's end, his full perfection, all that is truly human, all human aspiration, is fulfilled in relation to him. As John Paul II boldly declared in the first line of his first encyclical *Redemptor Hominis*: "The redeemer of man, Jesus Christ, is the center of the universe and of history."

To this point Albacete had embraced and personally promoted this Christocentrism—and that of allied thinkers like Hans Urs von Balthasar, Joseph Ratzinger, and Henri de Lubac—as the most adequate way to reconcile the disconnect between faith and life that plagued modern man. But in the encounter with Giussani, it became suddenly clear to him that something was lacking in his approach. No matter how profound or correct his theological response to modernity might be, as long as it remained at the level of theory—as long as it remained theology—it lacked the power to ignite change, to transform the Christian's engagement with the world.

This is where Giussani's years as a teacher at Berchet High School in Milan proved critical. His students knew the creed—they had been thoroughly catechized. But for them Jesus was a relic of the past, not "a present presence," as Giussani put it: he had no relation to their romances or their politics, their artistic passions or their scientific pursuits. Giussani saw that neither doctrine nor discourse were sufficient in and of themselves. For faith to become relevant, it had to be engaged in experience as an event—an encounter with a living person.

What Giussani proposed was a return to the central experience of Christianity, God's own method, summed up in the encounters that people have with Christ in the Gospels—John and Andrew, Zacchaeus, Mary Magdalene, the woman at the well. Jesus did not convince these men and women by discourse, but rather won them over through the power of his person, his gaze, his gestures, his presence. And each of these men and women experienced himself or herself as profoundly and humanly fulfilled in this concrete encounter—a meeting with *this* man, at *this* moment in time, in *this* precise place. As Albacete was to later say, paraphrasing Giussani: "Before becoming the center of the cosmos and of human history, Christ was a lump of blood in the womb of a woman."

Giussani re-proposed Christianity as something that was happening then and is still happening here and now in the Christian community, and in this way revivified the Christian experience for many. A movement was born. And now Albacete, already in his mid-fifties, found himself drawn toward it. He experienced Christ anew, alive, in the person of Luigi Giussani.

Looking back on this encounter, Albacete spoke not only of the beauty of the event but also its cost.

> I am proud to consider myself a son of Father Giussani. But making me find this towards the end of my life? I began to be even a little bit angry. The removal—the setting aside—of whatever theological knowledge I had in order to try out what Father Giussani was trying to teach me, was done because I knew that it was a fuller knowledge. I set this anger aside because this path led to amazement and for other reasons, it included the heart—the desires of the heart. The decision to try that out was a costly decision but it was a decision that I made willingly. Why? Because I am very saintly? No, because what is at stake is my ass. The future of my ass.

At Giussani's request, Albacete became a key agent in furthering the growth of Communion and Liberation in the U.S. and was made a national leader for the Fraternity of CL in 2000.

Over the next decade, he gave numerous talks inspired by Giussani's thought and guided CL's fledgling communities around the U.S., leading frequent retreats for both priests and laypersons. During this same period, he published *God at the Ritz*, a collection of *pensées* covering a wide range of subjects from the relationship between science and faith to politics, sexuality, and the meaning of suffering. Much of the book was the fruit of the conversations and encounters with his friends in the mainstream media.

When Albacete died in 2014, the outpouring of affection that emerged at that time—including tributes from commentators, churchmen, and scholars representing a range of political and religious viewpoints—gave evidence to his wide influence. Yet for all of his success as a writer and speaker, one thing Lorenzo Albacete did not possess was literary ambition. His columns, speeches, and essays were nearly always written at the request of various organizations and publications. They were often produced and delivered in the heat of a busy schedule, with no thought given to how they might eventually find an outlet in book form. So it has fallen to others to mine this material.

As editors, our charge has been to gather together in one place disparate pieces that offer a coherent survey of his vision. Most of the editorial work consisted in making the minor changes required to adapt talks intended to be heard into essays intended to be read. In a few places, we have felt free to rearrange some material or to add appropriate transitions—always in service of our mission to make Albacete's work find its way most directly into the hearts and minds of readers.

Without a doubt, this collection manifests Lorenzo Albacete's genius as the first thinker to fully translate Father Giussani's vision into an American cultural context and idiom. And he does it in his own brilliant, inimitable way, as an astronomer of the spirit, a companion of the Magi, who points us toward the love that Dante said "moves the sun and the other stars."

—Lisa Lickona & Gregory Wolfe

I. A POINT OF DEPARTURE

The Lovers and the Stars

Broadening Reason in an Age of Ideology

I have seen the stars.
I went up to the highest tree
In the whole poplar grove,
And saw thousands of eyes
In my own darkness.

GARCIA LORCA'S POEM "The Encounters of an Adventurous Snail" is about a rather serene snail, a gentleman of the forest who is not over-excited about anything. As he travels about, he runs into other animals. First he meets a bunch of frogs, who engage him in a very advanced discussion about the existence of God. By itself, that would have been fascinating to consider, but then he moves on, and runs into a bunch of ants. They are beating up one of their own and are about to kill her. "Ladies, what's wrong?" he asks. "What has she done? Why are you doing this?"

It turns out that this ant had disappeared from the colony for a time; while she was marching along she didn't see a tree coming, and when the tree arrived, she just went straight up the tree. She always looked only directly ahead, so when she was going up the tree, she could see the sky. For the first time in her life, she saw stars. She finally came down and could not hold in the news of what she had discovered, thinking (poor thing) that those who heard her would want to see the stars themselves.

Instead, they were furious. With this stupid talk about stars, she had broken the law of utility. The ant's usefulness, as it is for all members of an ant colony, is to be a worker, and she had interrupted that work by doing something the others considered absolutely outrageous, irrelevant, and stupid: looking at the stars.

Of course, the snail himself has no idea what stars are because he's never looked up either, but he's intrigued and asks the dying ant, "What are stars?" She has no words to describe them. "They're like little eyes," and they are very beautiful. Then she dies, and the other ants move on. The snail wonders about the meaning of what has happened, but he's just too tired to look up. Instead he continues his walk. In the distance you hear the bells of the church ringing.

It's a lovely poem, and it was a favorite of Monsignor Luigi Giussani. One day Giussani was walking around looking for a parking space, and he came upon two people making out in a car. He suddenly appeared in his cassock and said, "Hello." Well, you can imagine! When they saw him, he said, "I hate to interrupt; I just have one question to ask you: What you're doing now, what does it have to do with the stars?"

He had in mind this poem in which the stars represent infinity, the unknowable. He had in mind that our selves are constituted by relationship and that we can discover ourselves capable of an inexpressible relationship with infinity, with the mystery—with the stars.

I want to stick to this point of departure—the stars. I want to zero in on the very point where the subject becomes an interesting question, a determining factor in one's life. Gazing at the stars can awaken us to the unpleasantness and the inhumanity of the dualism in which we live—the kind of dualism that divides things like our faith and our work. Who wants to live such a life? Too much is needed to sustain this dualism, and along the way one of the sides tends to get ignored anyway.

Where does the reality of what we call "the stars"—the presence of the relationship of the mystery to us—enter into our human life, into our attempts to live a human life?

Following the teaching of Pope Benedict XVI, I have chosen the term "the broadening of reason" as a point of contact, the fruit of the impact between the stars and the human person. So I want to consider how what we call "reason" can be impacted by faith in the area of human love.

Everybody knows what affection is: affectivity. (Although I'm sure if you look up "affectivity," you'll find page after page of some kind of encyclopedia which will quickly remove your affectivity for the subject matter at hand.) It's sympathy. Affectivity is what happens when you say, "You know, that's good stuff." This "good stuff" has two aspects to it. First, it's a judgment; it's an affirmation of reason. *That's* good stuff. And second, it's an affirmation of affection, sympathy. Yeah, wow! That's *good* stuff. Reason and affectivity are very much interrelated in our daily experience, and therefore the broadening of reason must touch the broadening of affectivity.

What would it be like to have one's affectivity broadened? Again, we can search through our own experiences and see if there is something we can describe as a broadening, an intensification of affectivity. Are there experiences that make us care more about whatever is provoking the affectivity? The broadening of affectivity involves an increasing care, an increasing intensity. But remember, it should not be detached from reason. We should also experience an intensification in our ability to see what's there. And, in fact, affectivity does alter or impact what we see. It happens all the time. One guy comes to another guy and says that he has fallen in love—"I'm going crazy about her." And then the second guy says, "What the hell does he see in her?"

That's the point: he uses the word "see."

Let's go to *West Side Story*. Right before the song "Tonight," the word "see" comes up. Maria's concern is that when she looks at Tony she sees him as she does any other American, as a white person full of discrimination towards her because she's a dark Puerto Rican. But, in fact, with Tony, the experience is different. She tells him: "No, when I look at you, I see only you." And then he says, "See only me, Maria." And then she launches into the song. It is lovely stuff. Affectivity and seeing are inseparable.

The stars broaden what you see and intensify your caring about it, and in this sense guide it. When we speak about what guides our behavior we are talking about ethics, values. And the fact is that when we live according to an ethical system that doesn't correspond to our affectivity, it's a disaster. It's an imposed morality, inhuman.

So in the search for an ethical basis in the world to help us tame power and guide ourselves in ways that are not destructive of our humanity, the Church proposes this broadening of reason—and this necessarily involves the question of affectivity.

Immediately we run into a problem. In the cultural moment we are living, affectivity has been detached from reason. Our experience of "caring for"—our experience of meaning, of value, of purpose, of that which gives intelligibility to life and makes life worthwhile, the sense of destiny, what moves me—that reality has been separated from reason. And so in contemporary culture I discover two separate possibilities. One is the demand of pure, non-affective intelligence, and the other the pull of sheer, non-reasonable affectivity. In both cases, freedom disappears. We get first of all what John Paul II called "the tyranny of intelligence" and then the tyranny of emotions. The separation between reason and affectivity shows itself sooner or later in the manifestation of these two tyrannies.

I want to introduce another term. When they are operating in unison—when reason and affectivity are not separated—there occurs what we call *experience*. Experience is the way reality emerges in our consciousness. Reality becomes transparent when an authentic human experience occurs. Again, human experience is born of this wedding between reason and affectivity. Experience communicates to us the reality in which our presence is immersed. This is how that broadening occurs, by first becoming aware of the intensity of the real as something that has an impact on us, that we have encountered, that we did not create. The little ant who saw the stars knew very well they were not a product of her imagination. She had neither invented nor created them. Experience occurs because these two—reason and affectivity—remain together.

What happens next is the emergence, the taste, the grasping of real *otherness*. What is there is other. If these two, reason and affectivity, are separate, the experience of otherness is not possible. Everything becomes the projection of the self. It is the experience of otherness that is at the origin of the experience of responsibility. It is the recognition of this reality, grasped through reason and affectivity working together, that the sense of responsibility is born in me. If that experience is absent, if reason and affectivity have been separated, then responsibility is imposed on me.

But perhaps I'm scared by that, I would not like to say that; I want to consider myself basically a responsible person, an ethical person, so I try to do my best, through my own efforts. That's moralism. If it is not born from the real recognition of the other—an affective, reasonable recognition of the other—this disappearance of responsibility in the area of friendship and love shows itself in what the Bible calls "lust."

To get a better sense of what I mean, consider Karol Wojtyla's play, *Our God's Brother*. The main character Adam is struggling to get a sense of what responsibility means in the light of social injustice, in the light of his discovery that people are living in inhuman poverty in the places that he loves. This experience awakens his sense of responsibility, but he doesn't know what to do.

All kinds of people pop up with various proposals. According to the author, these are not real characters; these are aspects of Adam that he is working through within himself. One of them, "the Other," presents himself as a pure "intelligence." He describes himself: "I am an intelligence whose entire task is to reveal the true image of the world and not care for the rest."

"You too are an intelligence," he tells Adam. "That means you are subject to the laws of intelligence. . . . It is enough to hold the image of the world in your thoughts. You have no obligation to put its heavy burden on your back."

But Adam becomes aware of the limit of pure intelligence when he runs into a poor man reclining against a lamppost. He points the man out to the Other, but the Other cannot see him. Pure intelligence is not interested in this concrete individual. His gaze goes past him.

Adam says to him:

> There is a sphere in my thought that you do not possess. Which means that you do not grow out of my mind like my own thoughts. Ah, I have exposed you. I have done so with this image and likeness that you do not want to know.

This is a little fancy. Let's simplify it. The argument is that, aware of this "more"—the more that he has to see, know, take into account—Adam is able to resist these explanations that tempt him. Through the encounter with the poor, he has seen the stars, and he simply cannot get rid of that experience.

And pure intelligence is asking him to do just that. "I am an intelligence," he says. "That is enough for me." At this point, Adam says, "But the facts are against you. Do you see that man leaning against the lamppost?" And the Other says, "He does not attract my intelligence.

He has ceased to be an issue for me. I can go past him." Adam replies, "Oh how much is missing in you, how much you miss!"

Later on, when Adam is going to confession, he says to the priest, "My greatest temptation is the thought that one can love with the intelligence, with the intelligence only, and that this will suffice." The split between intelligence and affectivity, the reduction of what we call experience shows itself as a limitation of vision, as a narrowing. It doesn't allow us to see the concrete. It only allows us to see only the generic.

The difficulty we have in finding common ground for a way of life that responds to our affectivity and our sense of responsibility is a problem, says Giussani, that "is above all a crisis of reason." Until this is dealt with, a split will occur between the subject of action—I, myself, who I am—and reality, whether it's in politics, in economics, in science, or in personal relations. Our encounter with the stars—the birth of faith—addresses this problem and begins to heal it.

According to Giussani, we are suffering from three great reductions of reason.

In the first reduction, ideology—the abstract world of pure "intelligence"—prevents us from having a true experience of the event generated by our contact with reality. An event attracts our affectivity and reason, but when the split occurs, ideology takes the place of reason. Giussani describes ideology as "the logical discourse that starts with a prejudice and wishes to retain it and impose it." The experience of faith, the appearance of the stars, is a response. It comes from that discovery of otherness, from something that enters your life, an event. And it will free reason from this reduction to ideology. It will configure us—guide us, if you wish. It will configure a way of standing before reality. The way in which we look at it is an expansion of our looking, a change in our gaze before reality.

The second reduction is the reduction of the sign to mere appearance. A sign is when a reality you grasp, you see, points toward an other. The path of your deeper growth both in knowledge and affectivity is a moving from sign to sign. And the ability to grasp the sign, to follow a path, is the only way you will reach the mystery, since mystery is the depth of the sign. "Mystery," says Giussani, "becomes experience through the sign." But when the split occurs, the sign disappears. You might say that the sign fails to signify, remaining as it does at the level of an ever-changing superficiality, devoid of content. We are caught in the tyranny of appearance. When we have lost the ability to grasp the sign, then there's no reality that the sign points to, and the objectivity of the mystery, if you wish, also disappears, and the mystery question, the stars question, becomes pure abstract discussion.

Finally, the third reduction is a reduction of what the Bible calls the "heart" to pure feelings. The heart—the seat of our affectivity—rules over our personal dedication and fidelity. In this reduction, love becomes nothing more than sentimentality. But sentiments cannot guide us along the path of dedication and fidelity. Instead, the heart is precisely reason through objectivity. The broadening of reason intensifies, purifies our affectivity.

Again, affectivity—caring-for, attraction, sentiments—all of these can be brought together by talking about looking, about the way we look at reality. Our outlook—which literally means "looking out," the way I look away from myself—that is the stage, I propose to you, at which the impact between faith and affectivity takes place.

One of the best proposals of how the stars affect our looking on the level of affectivity, personal love relationships, is found in the now-famous book that was for many years ignored: *The Theology of the Body.* Although he wrote this before he was even pope, John Paul presented it over several years, as the content of his Wednesday audiences. Prior to this time, popes would generally use these weekly public moments to say a beautiful, inspired thing or two, but John Paul II sat there and read a philosophical treatise. I remember somebody asked him, "Aren't you concerned? Nobody understands anything." And he said, "They only come for the show. I can do that and in the meantime I get this stuff out, and it can be published."

At one point he discussed the words from the Sermon on the Mount when Jesus says that "Everyone who looks at a woman with lust has already committed adultery with her in his heart" (Mt 5:28). (Those of you who are old enough might remember that the phrase "adultery in the heart" was made popular by Jimmy Carter.) The pope examined the phrase "looking with lust." What does that mean? How does it happen? How do we get out of it?

He said two things: First of all, although in the Sermon on the Mount Jesus is speaking of a man looking at a woman with lust, it also applies in reverse; it also means a woman looking at a man with lust. Second, the teaching on adultery is not limited to a question of looking at somebody else who's not your wife, an extra-marital problem. Within marriage a husband can look at a wife with lust and vice-versa. And that is the same as adultery: it is adultery in the heart.

Well, when the Pope said that, the whole world reacted. "There the Catholic Church goes crazy once again against sexual pleasure. Now, even in marriage you can have sinful thoughts!" There were some serious editorials and some satirical columns making fun of the pope and the Church, so much so that the Vatican felt it had to issue a clarification.

But these points are important for what we are considering here. Listen to the words that describe this phenomenon of "looking with lust": "a deception of the human heart in the perennial call of man and woman." This perennial call is an "attraction," something we can consider without even mentioning men and women. We could say that "looking with lust" is a deception, a lack of the human heart in the personal call of love, "a call revealed in the mystery of creation—to communion by means of mutual giving." A call inscribed in the heart itself, the perennial attraction that occurs through a mutual gift of self—this is what is affected by lust. John Paul II calls it "an intentional 'reduction,' almost a restriction or closing down of the horizon of man and his heart."

This is amazing. The "heart" is the I, the self; it's everything. He is saying that lust closes the door to the horizon of man. It is a reduction of the other to being simply a suitable "object for gratification." It is the reduction of sexuality itself, an "obscuring of the significance of the body, and of the person itself." Femininity and masculinity thus cease being "a specific language of the spirit." They lose their "character of being a sign." And this reduction takes place, he says, "in the sphere of the purely interior act expressed by the look. A look... is in itself a cognitive act."

This is the heart of the problem. Because we have separated reason from affectivity, "looking" is separate from its cognitive dimension, the fact that it is an act of reason. Speaking of how we "look" at something, we say, "well, that's your perspective." Sight becomes a purely individual perspective. Whereas, John Paul II insists, "it is a cognitive act." It is the outcome of a judgment about reality.

This same thread is picked up in the first part of the encyclical *Deus Caritas Est*, in which Benedict XVI gives us a fascinating discussion of love. Human love begins with an attraction that always includes sexuality. It begins that way and it undertakes a path, a path that moves from sign to sign. In examining the two classical Greek words, *eros* and *agape*, he identifies precisely how faith begins to impact the experience of affectivity and love. For Benedict, the impression that our faith considers *eros* and *agape* as opposed is a misperception (although, it must be confessed, the Church has often expressed herself in such a way as to give that appearance). This was Nietzsche's great accusation against Christianity, that it had destroyed *eros*, the erotic, for the sake of the spiritual abstraction called *agape*—charity, love, divine love. Benedict says that isn't so. In fact, the purpose of revelation grasped by faith is the presence of the divine in the erotic, and—at this point I should veil my face—the presence of the human in the divine.

This is the proposal. It's where faith (the stars) enters in and broadens, purifies. Here it is proposed that what we call faith above all is the healing of our humanity. What we suffer from, whatever its origin, we must overcome this wound, this disaster, this separation of reason from affectivity.

If faith heals in some way, it will become manifest in the change it brings about in one's outlook and one's sense of responsibility. We will see reality in a different way. In *Our God's Brother*, a group of poor people become invisible to some. But others see them, and that seeing is accompanied by their caring. This is the origin of ethics. We see the same thing with concerns about the environmental crisis. Most people don't even see the crisis. But others see what is happening and they care. Faith brings about this deeper seeing and more intense caring, whether it is at the level of the environment or politics, or economics, or science—and certainly at the level of affective human relationships. The mystery and the stars—these words indicate the need to always go beyond.

Overcoming Dualism

Reason, Faith, Culture

YEARS AGO, I WORKED AT A physics lab. I was the only one there who claimed any belief in transcendence, not to mention Christianity or Catholicism. After a while, my colleagues asked me to explain myself. How was it that I could follow the scientific investigation of life with apparent interest and dedication and at the same time believe that a man who was dead popped out of the tomb two-and-a-half days later?

"You must be two different people," they said, "or one or the other is not true. These two dedications of the heart are incompatible." Notice how it was put. What is incompatible is the dedication of the heart, the worthwhile-ness of it. You cannot act out of interest in this area and the other one equally. You must be schizophrenic, a dualist.

Most of us are dualists. Most believers, most religious people, most Christians, most Catholics today are dualists. My awareness of this destructive, crippling, and mentally pathological dualism—because it is true that you cannot be two things that are radically opposed—forced me to seek an answer to my colleagues' question. I understood that what they were bringing up is a conflict between two cultures—the scientific culture, with its distinctive *logos*, and that of the faith, with its own rationality. I became interested in the question of faith and culture.

Fortunately, at the Second Vatican Council, the Church had already grappled with this question, the issue of the encounter between the Church and contemporary culture. The council's Declaration on the Church in the Modern World, *Gaudium et Spes*, led me directly to the anthropological dimension of the problem. The apparent conflict between the Church and culture could be resolved only by an adequate view of what the human person is, an "adequate anthropology," as John Paul II was going to call it many years later. *Gaudium et Spes* concludes its analysis with a statement that became a favorite quote of John Paul II: *Gaudium et Spes*, 22. Bluntly put, what is asserted is that the only reason that human beings exist, the only reason I exist, is so that Christ might exist—as Saint Paul says, "so that he might be the firstborn among many brothers" (Rom 8:29). And the only reason that Christ exists, the only reason there is an Incarnation—by Christ I mean Jesus, not the eternal *Logos*—is so that we might exist.

In practical terms this means that everything human that is interesting can lead me to Christ. Any manifestation of authentic humanity—human works, human relationships, human dreams, human fears, and even human sins—is linked to Jesus Christ because there is no human reality without Christ. The human, the real, the world we build and the one in which we live—that is a path, *the* path of the human heart to Jesus Christ. The link is between Jesus and the real.

In his 2007 speech at Aparecida, Brazil, to the Latin American Bishops Conference, Pope Benedict XVI addressed this link. You must understand the drama of the occasion. In Latin America, the inability of faith to generate a culture that reflected the Christian reality was obvious. There was a desperate need to change a culture that sustained scandals, that structurally sustained the gap between abysmal poverty and riches. If Christianity had nothing to offer against this, or, even worse, was somehow tied to it, then it had to go.

So the Church faced quite an issue. It was not unlike what Luigi Giussani faced in 1954 when he realized that the reconstruction of the post-war culture in Italy was not generating a genuinely Catholic culture despite churches filled with the Catholic faithful. What does Christianity bring to this world, to life, to culture? Does it matter? What happens in this world where Christianity is lived?

Liberation theology attempted to answer these questions in Latin America by proposing an analysis of the situation and a method to deal with it, and all of it linked to Christ. It seemed to be exactly what was needed. But then it met a Roman resistance, led by John Paul II through the ministry of Joseph Ratzinger. And now Joseph Ratzinger, as Pope, was going to Latin America. It was a dramatic moment, the kind of situation in which one does not whip out a speech with all the usual stuff. Benedict must have thought about it with great care, not only because of the risk of confusing people, but above all because many people there had risked their lives and were risking their lives for something that did not appear to have the support of the Church.

The question, says Benedict, is:

> What does Christ actually give us? Why do we want to be disciples of Christ? The answer is: because, in communion with him, we hope to find life, the true life that is worthy of the name, and thus we want to make him known to others, to communicate to them the gift that we have found in him. Is it really so? Are we really convinced that Christ is the way, the truth, and the life? In the face of the priority of faith in Christ, and of life in him, a further question could arise: could this priority not perhaps be a flight towards emotionalism, towards religious individualism, an abandonment of the urgent reality of the great economic, social, and political problems of Latin America and the world, and a flight from reality towards a spiritual world?

He has landed in the same spot we have landed.

> What is real? Are only material goods, social, economic, and political problems "reality"? This was precisely the great error of the dominant tendencies of the last century, a most destructive error, as we can see from the results of both Marxist and capitalist systems. They falsify the notion of reality by detaching it from the foundational and decisive reality which is God. Anyone who excludes God from his horizons falsifies the notion of "reality" and, in consequence, can only end up in blind alleys or with recipes for destruction.

The first basic point to affirm, then, is the following: only those who recognize God know reality and are able to respond to it adequately and in a truly human manner.

> Yet here a further question immediately arises: who knows God? How can we know him? We cannot enter here into a complex discussion of this fundamental issue. For a Christian, the nucleus of the reply is simple: only God knows God, only his Son who is God from God, true God, knows him. And he "who is nearest to the Father's heart has made him known" (Jn 1:18). Hence the unique and irreplaceable importance of Christ for us, for humanity. If we do not know God in and

with Christ, all of reality is transformed into an indecipherable enigma; there is no way, and without a way, there is neither life nor truth.

Later on, almost exactly following Giussani's approach, the Pope underlines that this waking up of our hearts to reality is what salvation means. To be saved is to know the real. That certainly includes the drama of our sins and their consequences and our redemption from them—but it is so much broader. Usually we restrict Christianity to only that drama: salvation is just salvation from hell. But salvation is fundamentally the heart's recognition of the real; therefore, it's part of the drama of creation, independently of how it is shaped by the power of sin.

But it is not enough to end where I've just ended: Christ and the real. The question is, so now what? Where is this Christ? Where does this happen? If there is a connection between Christ and the real, and they are inseparable, then any increase in one leads to the other. An experience of the presence of Christ will make you passionately fascinated by what is real—by the little flower, the cosmos, the macrocosm, the microcosm, even accounting at Merrill Lynch. Conversely, if you know that, if you follow that passionate fascination, the path will lead you to Christ. Pursuing that path of your interest will lead you to Christ.

That's the claim. So, the next question is: How is it verified? "Always be ready," says Saint Peter, "to give an explanation to anyone who asks you for a reason for your hope" (1 Pet 3:15). An encounter with Christ will lead to an interest and a passion and a love for reality that will surprise us because that thirst is what defines the human heart, and that doesn't age. When the heart encounters Christ, that thirst comes out from within you with the same force that it could have when you were fifteen years old—only you're now sixty-six. The link with eternity does not change. All of those desires are activated. The religious sense is jump-started and headed in the right direction, and it shows itself again in an interest in all that exists.

There are other signs, but to me this one is fundamental in the way we face the culture. The culture is defined in terms of how we look at and experience reality. The real choice is between a dualism that separates the sacred and the secular—the flesh and the spirit—and a unified, incarnational vision. All of this is sustained by the grace of the encounter with Christ. It's unexpected, but it isn't a purely mental operation, or purely spiritual. It occurs through someone in a given place, at a given time. Fidelity to that particularity is essential because that keeps us within the orbit of the encounter, sustaining our approach to the real. Christians are not here to show a specifically Catholic genius or to engage in a battle. We are here to give witness to our faith, yes, but also to really to live with the confidence that that same faith gives us, to understand what is real, what is being seen, what is being lived. Again, this awakens interest, and with interest, light. This is the only way.

The Church of the Infinitely Fractured

Nihilism and the Search for Communion

IN A *HARPER'S* ESSAY published in 2007, Curtis White addresses what he calls the "Gnostic character" of the soup we call Christianity in the United States today. The article's subtitle is "Hot Air Gods," the pejorative term the prophets Isaiah and Jeremiah use for pagan idols.

When we assert "This is my belief," says White, we are invoking our right to have our own private conviction, no matter how ridiculous, not only tolerated politically, but respected by others. It says, "I've invested a lot of emotional energy in this belief, and in a way I've staked the credibility of my life on it. So if you ridicule it, you can expect a fight."

In this kind of culture, "Yahweh and Baal—my God and yours—stroll arm-in-arm, as if to do so were the model of virtue itself." Baal stands for everything that was considered idolatrous by the Jews in the pagan world, and Yahweh, the one and only true God. These days, they get along very well.

White continues:

> What we require of belief is not that it make sense but that it be sincere. This is so even for our more secular convictions. . . . Clearly, this is not the spirituality of a centralized orthodoxy. It is a sort of workshop spirituality that you can get with a cereal-box top and five dollars. And yet in our culture, to suggest that such belief is not deserving of respect makes people anxious, an anxiety that expresses itself in the desperate sincerity with which we deliver life's little lessons. . . . There is an obvious problem with this form of spirituality: it takes place in isolation. Each of us sits at our computer terminal tapping out

our convictions. . . . Consequently, it's difficult to avoid the conclusion that our truest belief is the credo of heresy itself. It is heresy without an orthodoxy. It is heresy as an orthodoxy.

This getting along between Yahweh and Baal leads to a spiritual life "in isolation." It makes an authentic community—in which people share the original insights that give meaning to their lives—impossible. A community may appear, but it is a community of isolated individuals, that is to say, a community sustained by the very same reality that communities are meant to break through. That isolation becomes the orthodoxy. The fact that there is no unifying set of convictions brings everyone together in the task of making sure they don't hurt each other. It is a community built on heresy. "It is heresy as orthodoxy."

When the political freedom of religion has been broadened to the dogma that

> everyone is free to believe whatever she likes, there is no real shared conviction at all, and hence no church and certainly no community. Strangely, our freedom to believe has achieved the condition that Nietzsche called nihilism, but by a route he never imagined.

While European nihilists just denied God, "American nihilism is something different. Our nihilism is our capacity to believe in everything and anything all at once. It's all good!"

> We would prefer to be left alone, warmed by our beliefs-that-make-no-sense, whether they are the quotidian platitudes of ordinary Americans, the magical thinking of evangelicals, the mystical thinking of New Age Gnostics, the teary-eyed patriotism of social conservatives, or the perfervid loyalty of the rich to their free-market Mammon. We are thus the congregation of the Church of the Infinitely Fractured, splendidly alone together. And apparently that's how we like it. Our pluralism of belief says both to ourselves and to others, "Keep your distance."

White concludes:

> And yet isn't this all strangely familiar? Aren't these the false gods that Isaiah and Jeremiah confronted, the cults of the "hot air gods"? The gods that couldn't scare birds from a cucumber patch? Belief of every kind and cult, self-indulgence and

self-aggrandizement of every degree, all flourish. And yet God
is abandoned.

These are the reflections of a non-Christian on what he calls
"Christ-less Christianity."

My first question in front of this: can the freedom we believe that
Catholic orthodoxy—Catholic truth—makes possible, be achieved
living in this culture? Or should we separate from the dominant culture and recreate something that we liked better in the past, build walls
around it, and wait to see what happens in the future, stepping out
now and then to see if the situation has improved or to send out agents
to infiltrate? What do we propose to everyone?

One of the responses to this question is to present Christianity
fundamentally as a source of ethics. We respond to "Christ-less Christianity" by helping society recall the values, the ethics, upon which it
was once built.

But is the proper response an ethical one? Is the best response
to present society with an ethical proposal that will bring everyone together?

In the appropriately titled *Christless Christianity: The Alternative
Gospel of the American Church*, Michael S. Horton addresses this very
point. Horton critiques the practice of using Gospel stories, whether
Old Testament or New, as moral parables meant to apply to our lives.
This, he says, evacuates their power as saving stories:

> Instead of drawing a straight line of application from the nar-
> rative to us, which typically moralizes or allegorizes the story,
> we are taught by Jesus himself to understand these passages in
> light of their place in the unfolding drama of redemption that
> leads to Christ. . . . Moralistic preaching, the bane of conserva-
> tives and liberals alike, assumes that we're not really helpless
> sinners that need to be rescued, but decent folks who just
> need a few good examples, exhortations, and instructions.

Horton quotes Australian theologian Grahame Goldsworthy, who argues:

> We are not saved by our changed lives. The changed life is the
> result of being saved and not the basis of it. The basis of salva-
> tion is the perfection in the life and death of Christ presented
> in our place. . . . By reverting to either allegorical interpretation

on the one hand, or to prophetic literalism on the other, some Evangelicals have thrown away the hermeneutical gains of the Reformers in favor of a medieval approach to the Bible. . . . Evangelicals have had a reputation for taking the Bible seriously. But even they have traditionally propagated the idea of the short devotional reading from which a blessing from the Lord must be wrested.

Goldsworthy concludes:

The pivotal point of turning in Evangelical thinking which demands close attention is the change that has taken place from the Protestant emphasis upon the objective facts of the gospel in history, to the medieval emphasis on the inner life.

So here is the problem with the reduction of our proposal to ethics, to an ethical way of life. As both of these authors show, it's not Christianity. Christianity begins with the experience of being saved and then seeks to live that experience in the surrounding culture in all its defining points—at work, in human relations, in politics, in economics, and so on.

It is not the other way around: you don't reform those areas in order to be saved, but you give witness to being saved. The saving initiative of God in Christ comes first. That is to say, what saves us are the facts of the life of Christ and of his death and resurrection, not the ethical consequences drawn from them by the right wing or the left wing. This sense was the heart of the Protestant Reformation, and it has been lost by the vast majority of Protestants, as evidenced in their interpretation of the Bible as an inspiring source of moral behavior, both for left- and right-wing purposes.

It is interesting that Goldsworthy, in arguing on behalf of the purity of the Reformation, says that the problem is that the Catholic Church is guilty of moralism because we have emphasized the inner life. Just when you think that he is on the verge of giving a Catholic criticism of this view, it turns out the Catholic Church is as guilty of it as the mainstream Protestant churches and the Evangelical fundamentalists. The accusation here is that at a certain point around the Middle Ages the Catholic Church began to emphasize the inner life and progress in faith became identified with progress in one's inner life. As an authentic Protestant, Goldsworthy sees this as a great error that demands reform. The whole point of the Reformation was that the point of departure of the Christian life is the events that bring about our salvation. Because of original sin, we do not have the inner strength or the inclination to make these changes by ourselves.

What are we Catholics to make of this criticism? Is the Catholic Church today substituting inner life experiences for the facts of history that brought about our salvation? And has this crippled the Church's capacity to respond to the nihilistic culture?

One way to judge this is to consider something that Catholics and Protestants hold in common. Christianity exists because an initiative was taken by God. For Protestants, the only source for this initiative is the Bible. And the Catholic Church concurs that the Bible is the "Word of God," that is to say that through the reading of the Bible, the proclamation of the Bible, we are being spoken to by God. The Word of God is not information about God; it is a call from God.

Pope Benedict XVI takes up this point in his book *Jesus of Nazareth*. He says that the purpose of his study, and indeed the purpose of biblical hermeneutics of interpretation, is to discover more and more how the unifying reality of the Bible, with all its diversity and even contradictions, is the *Gestalt* of Jesus Christ. And a Catholic way to approach the Bible is to read it in the light of the desire to know better, to discover more about, to see more clearly, the *Gestalt* of Jesus of Nazareth.

In an article on Benedict's study, Adrian J. Walker suggests that there is a slight problem with this word *Gestalt* as used by the pope. *Gestalt* is translated into English as "figure." The "*Gestalt* of Jesus of Nazareth" is "the figure of Jesus of Nazareth." But, Walker argues, *Gestalt* means much more than just "figure"; it's akin to "weight" in the Johannine sense. It suggests the glory—the power—of a presence. The *Gestalt* is the shape of the personality, the taste of it. It's not just an image; it is a powerful presence.

When I first met Pope John Paul II, he was having breakfast and stuffing himself with Corn Flakes. He was a powerful presence even without the usual props. He had a weight of a presence and it was not produced by show business. You could get any Mickey Mouse to come out on a balcony in white and look impressive. He didn't need this. His humanity had that weight. That was his *Gestalt*. It was the same for Mother Teresa, whom I met at a lunch with a bunch of beautiful-looking cardinals. When she came into the room all of these other dignitaries suddenly shrank in size. She who was physically a little thing showed a tremendous weight of presence.

This is what we look for when we read sacred scripture: the weight of his presence. Walker calls this reading scripture with a "Christocentric hermeneutic." This way of reading that reveals more and more of the *Gestalt* of Christ is what creates the canon of sacred scripture. Jesus Christ, his power of presence, is the interpretation of scripture. As Jesus says in the Gospel of John, "I am the grammar of Moses."

Here's the first thing we can propose in this moment: a life that seeks to discover the attraction of the *Gestalt* of Jesus. There are two symptoms that indicate progress in our experience of discovering the *Gestalt* of Jesus. One is simply our expanding interest in the human and all its expressions. And the other is a certain joy—a joy that is completely compatible with and in fact so often tied to suffering and pain and even emotional disgust at the injustices we have to face. When we refuse to look away from the most horrific scenes, but instead face them, seeing even there the *Gestalt* of Jesus, we experience something that, for lack of a better word, we call joy—something seemingly totally incompatible with disgust at the injustice. We see it in Christ himself confronting the death of Lazarus and his reaction to the son of the widow of Nain. First he cries. There's no question he's disgusted by what he sees, and yet he works a miracle that shows the power of his presence.

In the end, it seems to me that White's criticism of American nihilism and of the Christianity that characterizes the majority of Americans today is basically correct. And the Protestants who agree with his criticism are right: the inner life, the spiritual life, has taken the place of the "event," to use Giussani's term. But although this criticism may be intellectually correct and even brilliant, it remains merely a discourse. It doesn't move anyone. What is missing is what Giussani indicates: "The experience of Jesus is a saving event here and now, in my life, at this moment, at this place. Because if that is not present, then everything really remains an abstraction about the past. Jesus is a museum figure." Or, as he says, "Jesus will have failed."

The Protestant misses this aspect of the here and now. What is missing is a sacramental view of reality and therefore the Church, because it is through the sacrament that the here and now occurs within the life of the Church. Before it narrows further to a particular charism, it is the community that keeps us together, *this* way of living the sacramental nature of the Church. Finally, only this orientation to reality will, through sheer grace and the love of God, allow the *Gestalt* of Jesus to appear today, here and now, in this world of ours, and dispel the doubts that obscure.

Searching for Truth Together

Monasticism as a Movement

I READ POPE BENEDICT'S "Address at the Meeting with Representatives from the World of Culture at the Collège des Bernardins" the day after it was given, and I have since come to believe that this is one of the most important addresses to come from any pope in modern times. In it, Benedict claims that the way monastic culture was born is revealing of how Christianity is defined. He addresses what it means to be a Christian for all times and offers a method of looking at reality that is also at the heart of Giussani's work and charism. He proposes what is, in essence, *the* Christian method.

The monks were responding to their set of circumstances, and we have our own. But we share the same underlying background: the collapse of certainties. And so it is crucial for those who are concerned about the relation between our faith and culture to consider his words.

The monks, Benedict claims, were brought together by their shared experience of ideological and cultural confusion. This underlying experience gave rise to a question: in the midst of this confusion, what can you depend on? They were motivated by what we would call a desire for truth. Thus the beginning of monastic culture was what Fr. Giussani would call "the formation of a movement"—a people coming together to pursue the search for truth together.

"It was not their intention," says Benedict, "to create a culture nor even to preserve a culture from the past. Their motivation was much more basic. The goal was *quaerere Deum*." They were searching for God.

This was neither a pietistic nor an escapist response:

Amid the confusion of the times, in which nothing seemed permanent, they wanted to do the essential—to make an effort to find what was perennially valid and lasting, life itself. They were searching for God. They wanted to go from the inessential to the essential, to the only truly important and reliable thing there is. It is sometimes said that they were "eschatologically" oriented. But this is not to be understood in a temporal sense, as if they were looking ahead to the end of the world or to their own death, but in an existential sense: they were seeking the definitive behind the provisional.

In the midst of confusion in which everything was falling apart, the monks sought the essential, namely that which has value and remains, that which is trustworthy. What was important in the midst of these confusing circumstances was to find life, life itself.

And what was life to them? Human life. Looking for God was not a pious goal or an escape into the unchanging mystery that offers protection from the waves of confusion; it was rather to enter into these waves of confusion and to discover there what remains, what survives, what has value, what is worthwhile to live for. Following the tradition, Benedict calls this an eschatological orientation, not in the sense of that which comes after the end—either the end of the world or the end of one's individual life—but in the sense of that which has value in life in the present. They were looking for (and I love this phrase) "the definitive in the midst of the provisional."

Though they were motivated by this experience of unrest, this desire for truth, their point of departure, was not this experience. They were Christians; they believed that God had revealed the method to find him and cleared the path to him. So, their first task was to understand revelation well, to understand their faith well. They were convinced that the faith is true and wanted to see what it implies, what it means in terms of how to judge the present situation and how to respond to it.

For the monks, this faith was centered on the word, the *logos*. The *logos* is not at all merely an intellectual concept, but a reality that catches our attention, that is addressed to us. It is what Giussani would call an encounter. It is a call; it is therefore a vocation. Human life itself was experienced as a response to a word addressed in human words; life became a response to this encounter with the Word.

A "culture of the word" developed. And since revelation occurs through communication among humans, one studies human communication, how human beings speak in narratives, in poetry, in myths. They wanted to penetrate "the secret of language," the structure of human language, the models and modes of expression that human beings have. And this led them further, to the study of what humanity itself means. Only thus could they recognize the impact of the presence of the divine *Logos*—how it is speaking to them and what it is saying.

Benedict has a lovely French expression for all of this: *L'amour des lettres,* "love for letters." Call it a culture of the word, a love for the human. "Letters" here stands for everything. The reason "letters" is used is because revelation is seen in terms of words. For Giussani, revelation is experienced when you encounter a different kind of humanity, one that provokes your curiosity. In the midst of your search for meaning, big or small, a sudden encounter strikes you. This changed humanity is the same thing as the monastic word *logos.* In what does this difference consist? What does it mean to be human? We need not restrict it to just words. The reason it's in those terms for the monks is because of the *logos,* their point of departure.

This created a need to know the human sciences. The monks did not have the technology, the studies, the advantages that we have; nevertheless they devoted the best of their efforts to what the sciences were saying about what it means to be human.

And so another reality sprang from *L'amour des lettres:* a library. The monks collected as much of the written wisdom as they could. And once they had the human sciences, the study of communication, and a library, they started schools. The monastic movement became a school of God's service—*dominici schola servitii*—a school in which one is taught how to find the truth in the midst of confusion, how to find the truth of life. The school served what was called *eruditio.* Perhaps this is the best expression of all: it was a school for the formation of reason.

This search started with an unexpected personal provocation, and while the path always remains personal, at the same time, when the *Logos* enters into human words, into the human reality, it points one toward community. This is, if you will, the first consequence of following this method: the rest of your search has to be conducted within a community, not by yourself. "The word does not lead to a purely individual path of mystical immersion," but introduces us to a communion with those walking by faith, "to the pilgrim fellowship of faith." And here we are touching on the very nature of reality: the question of the Trinity, the secret life of the mystery being love, and the Church as an expression of this community.

A second consequence: the search cannot be purely intellectual. It requires what Benedict calls "corporal acts." When an event surpasses the categories in which it can be explained, it can come to us only through our engagement with a symbol, with ritual. In his 2009 Easter Vigil homily, Benedict highlighted three such moments in the Easter liturgy. First, the Easter candle: he discusses candles and what they are made of, how they give light by dying, the meaning of light. He appeals to our total involvement in the experience of the candle. (A cheap Easter candle weakens your awareness of the Resurrection.)

The second symbol is the baptismal water, and you can go on forever with the symbolic connections: the sea, the river's death, new life, freshness, thirst (and Benedict does go on). You cannot baptize someone by saying, "Imagine that you are sinking in that water," while they are still standing up.

The third aspect of the Easter liturgy that Benedict brings forward is singing. (I tried it in my parish and Jesus went back into the tomb.) But the concern about singing correctly, about the beauty of song, is not optional. The word teaches us how to speak with God and the paradigm of this was the Psalms. Remember, Benedict cautions us, the Psalms begin with singing instructions that are not arbitrary to the meaning of the Psalm. The music is required to pray, to converse with the Word of God. Merely pronouncing it is not sufficient.

In the Address at the Collège des Bernardins, Benedict references Psalm 138:1: "In the presence of the angels, I will sing for you, O Lord." And he adds, "What this expresses is the awareness that in communal prayer one is singing in the presence of the angels." In this context, the confusion that the monks experienced—that confusion outside—is seen as a disharmony, and it is music that conveys the experience of harmony that allows you to escape or to see better the disharmony around you.

Benedict quotes Saint Augustine, who speaks of his life before his conversion as a "zone of dissimilarity." Augustine was living in the region of disharmony. In this case redemption is experienced as the reestablishment of harmony.

The challenge is to learn how to sing along with the music of creation itself. And so the underlying problem here is the restoration of the harmony of creation. And in scripture itself and in the Fathers, this extends even to nature. This is not something we make up. Consider this passage from Abraham Joshua Heschel's *The Earth is the Lord's: The Inner World of the Jew in Eastern Europe*.

> Even the landscape became Jewish. In the month of Elul during the penitential season, the fish in the streams trembled. On Lag ba-Omer, the scholars' festival in the spring, all the trees rejoiced. When a holiday came, even the horses and dogs felt it. And the crow perched on a branch looked from a distance "as though it were wearing a white prayer shawl with dark blue stripes in front, and it sways and bends as it prays, and it lowers its head in intense supplication."

Now, recall that this consideration of the "corporal acts," the symbols, is all to the purpose of understanding the text of scripture, the Word expressed in human words, because that indeed is the source of the proclamation of what Christianity is all about. These are the tools that will allow us to make sense of what otherwise appears an impossible problem, namely, to find the principle of unity in the scriptures, writings that are a thousand years in the making. Is there an interior unity among them? In what does it lie? What about the path from the Old Testament to the New Testament? What is the principle of unity that somehow or other does not destroy the discontinuity between the two? Again, this is a serious task of reason, armed by all the community, the gestures, the singing—all of it helping reason along on its task of discovering the presence of the divine in the human.

This is Benedict's crucial point: "The unity of the biblical books and the divine character of their words cannot be grasped by purely historical methods." You cannot be looking for unity in purely historical terms or in terms of human communication because human communications are *human* communications. "The letter indicates the facts and events," says Saint Augustine. The message, "what you have to believe, is indicated by allegory," by immersion into a world of symbols. It's amazing. The Christological and pneumatological dimension of scripture can be discovered only after an adequate "exegesis," an interpretation, a work of reason—and for this the community is essential. A community was formed precisely by the Word within the words, and thus entering this community releases the capacity of your reason to do an adequate exegesis.

Christianity, therefore, is not strictly speaking a religion of the book. Christianity captures the Word, the *Logos* in the words, to spread this mystery through this multiplicity, the reality of a human history, the history of this community. In that sense the structure of the Bible is a challenge to each generation. This is also why fundamentalism is not allowed, is not a solution. Another way of saying it is that the Word is not already present in the literalness of the Bible. It is not already locked in, such that simply reading it releases it. To reach it, a transcending process of comprehension is necessary, guided by an interior movement, a process of living. "Only within the dynamic unity of the whole are the many books really *one* book."

The method, the Christian method, includes the text, the words, the community, its history, how it has lived this revelation. Without this we will not grasp the Word, the *Logos*, and therefore will miss what we were looking for to begin with—the definitive, the worthwhile, the valuable, in the midst of this disharmony.

II. AMERICA AND MODERNITY

Standing in Solomon's Portico

America's Debate about Freedom

FOR THE PAST THREE YEARS in New York City, I have been meeting with a group of American progressives from the media, the academy, the literary world, and political organizations. I met these friends when I was working on an article on Pope John Paul II and Fidel Castro for *The New Yorker*, and an opinion column for *The New York Times* on the Pope's vision of a unified continental "American" Catholic Church, as well as during my work as consultant on Catholic matters to PBS. As a result, they invited me to join their group, representing, I suppose, the "view from eternity."

You might say that I have been standing in "Solomon's Portico"—that portion of the Temple in Jerusalem where people would gather to engage in conversation about serious matters—as the apostles of Jesus were said to do after the Ascension.

In the midst of all this I have received a brand-new mystical gift appropriate to the new millennium. Perhaps you have heard of "bi-location," the extraordinary gift given to certain mystics and saints (like Padre Pio, for example) to be in two places at the same time. I don't understand these things, but I am not that amazed by it since, as a former physicist, I became acquainted with even stranger behavior at the sub-atomic level. Moreover, being in more than one place at the same time is really quite common today in the world of email, cellular phones, and the internet.

But the really extraordinary mystical gift that I have received is the gift of no-location, that is, the ability to be in no place at all. If I cannot be located through phone calls, faxes, emails, etc., it is because I am probably in the midst of one of these mystical disappearances.

I was thinking of this when I read recently that most Americans today call themselves "ideological moderates," choosing this term over "liberal" and "conservative." This new ideology provides a political home for no-location mystics, since it enshrines in a political philosophy the refusal to think through and judge. Ideological moderation is the ability to be totally and blissfully above all concrete issues, the ideology of non-thinking, the commitment to non-commitment, the party of no-party.

I am not the only one to notice this, as you can see in a cartoon published in *The New Yorker*. It shows a modern-day version of Patrick Henry, a famous promoter of the American Revolution against Britain. He is the author of the celebrated cry: "Give me liberty or give me death!" In this cartoon you see a political leader in what seems to be a campaign appearance, and he has his hand raised high in a dramatic gesture, exclaiming: "Give me moderation, or give me death." It is funny, but it is also sad: is this what the American devotion to liberty has come to mean today? From Patrick Henry to ideological moderation?

I do not think this is yet the case, but it is a danger, and my hope in the meetings with my friends is that American liberalism will be strong enough to struggle against this danger.

In *The Story of American Freedom*, Eric Foner maintains,

> No idea is more fundamental to Americans' sense of themselves as individuals and as a nation than freedom. The central term in our political vocabulary. . . is deeply embedded in the documentary record of our history and the language of everyday life. The Declaration of Independence lists liberty among mankind's inalienable rights; the Constitution announces as its purpose to secure liberty's blessings. The Civil War was fought to bring forth "a new birth of freedom," World War II for the "Four Freedoms" and the Cold War to defend the Free World. . . . If asked to justify their actions, public or private, Americans are likely to respond, "It's a free country."

Of course, when asked to define what freedom or liberty means, we will find as many definitions as there are differences in desires as well as fears. Most would say: "Freedom is the ability to do what

I desire, as well as the protection from what other individuals might desire that will threaten my freedom."

This underlines an important point: American history follows no particular definition of freedom. On the contrary, American history should be seen as a tension, a competition, or even a violent struggle between different understandings of freedom. What is common to all is the radical attraction of the ideal itself: everyone understands freedom as the ideal or value with which to judge the correspondence with the national identity and mission of all proposed courses of political action.

Foner calls freedom in the United States an "essentially contested concept," a concept that by its very nature is the subject of disagreement. It automatically presupposes an on-going dialogue with other, competing meanings. What unites the country politically, then, is an agreement to follow the rules for the competition between the different forms of freedom, as well as an agreement on the way to change the rules when necessary.

Two things must be said about this. First, this view of the situation is different from the so-called "procedural republic" model. According to this view, the state should be absolutely neutral with respect to a specific philosophical or religious notion of freedom. Each citizen, individually or in a free association with others, sets for himself or herself the good or goods that define his or her view of personal fulfillment. The state should not favor any particular view of the individual or common good. It should simply set and defend the procedures that secure this neutrality and facilitate the pursuit of the many freely chosen individual goods. One of these conditions is equality of opportunity, and the state does have the obligation to assure it.

Such philosophical or religious neutrality is impossible. It is itself a philosophical, and even religious, option. It expresses an anthropology that does not correspond with the human experience of what is true and just. Viewing freedom as an essentially contested concept or value, however, does not rule out a political promotion of individual and common goods based on philosophical or religious choice. It merely recognizes that in a pluralist society no particular philosophical or religious position will ever fully correspond to the experience of all the people about what is good and true. In this case, the "rules of the game" will allow competition between the different conceptions of freedom, with the state assuring that as many citizens as possible will enjoy the opportunity to compete.

Second, I do not deny that the view of freedom as an essentially contested concept is indeed itself a philosophical (and even religious) choice in that it betokens a particular anthropological view. But in my opinion—given the impossibility of a truly neutral or content-free position—the anthropology behind this view corresponds with an experience common to all, namely conflict or tension in the human heart. In fact, this tension—this polarity—is constitutive of the human person whose fundamental or original desires seek a unity between apparently contradictory directions.

Hans Urs von Balthasar identifies the three constitutive human polarities as spiritual and physical, male and female, and individual and community. Indeed, the last two are expressions of the first. That the human being is both limited and unlimited, temporal and eternal, can be discovered through a rational analysis of the most fundamental desires of the human heart, and this is the basis for what is called the religious sense—that is, the experience of dependence on a transcendent mystery at the origins and destiny of human experience. Indeed, as Luigi Giussani has insisted, freedom is the human link with the infinite, and this is expressed precisely in the experience of these polarities. Since freedom is the link with a transcendent mystery, no one definition of it will ever capture its full meaning, nor could it ever be given a single political expression.

From the very beginning, the framework within which the debate about freedom has taken place in American history has been a Protestant vision of the world. The "moral" or "Christian" view of freedom dominated in the pre-Revolutionary Anglo-American world: freedom as self-reliance, self-control, the strength to live by Biblical ethical standards. The Anglo-American Protestant world was seen as the divinely chosen home of freedom in a world sunk into savagery or held in bondage by tyranny. Another word for tyranny was "popery." Protestantism meant freedom; Catholicism meant tyranny. Even when a secularized notion of freedom replaced the Protestant theological one, this framework remained. Freedom was seen as the capacity of the Anglo-American Protestant citizens to live life according to a "rule of law," in contrast with the "servile" subjects of Catholic countries.

Later, even England was held to have been corrupted, leaving the "New England" as the chosen beacon of human freedom.

Amazingly, this dimension of the freedom debate is present even to contemporary times. I remember the controversy in the Republican primary in South Carolina, when George W. Bush decided to accept an award from Bob Jones University, a fundamentalist Protestant school where inter-racial dating was prohibited on Biblical grounds, and where the rector of the university held Catholicism to be a Satanic religion and the Pope to be the Anti-Christ.

I also remember listening to a popular talk-radio-program in the New York City area, as the host, a conservative Irish-American Catholic, was amazed to discover the number of callers living in this—the most cosmopolitan and pluralistic region of the world—who defended this position. Interestingly, these people, as well as the authorities of Bob Jones University, see this as an expression of freedom. This university, for example, is one of the very few in the country that flourishes without one cent of federal financial help. This too is characteristic of this view of freedom: it tends to consider government power as threatening. This has been a consistent dimension of the American debate about freedom.

This dimension of freedom leads to another that has been a constant thread in the American debate, namely freedom as the participation in political authority. This participation, however, required evidence of the moral capacity to exercise it responsibly, and this was one of the reasons for the limitation of this right to property owners and the exclusion of women and non-whites (and African Americans, Native Americans, and Asians). One of the main lines of historical development in the American history of freedom has been the challenge of extending this right to more and more citizens—an effort that even led to a civil war.

The American Revolution begins this process of the "democratization of freedom," although at the beginning the rebels appealed to British principles for vindication of their cause. When England ignored this appeal, the colonists began to see America as the bearer of humankind's quest for freedom.

This appeal to humankind was to lead to the Declaration of Independence's appeal to natural rights as the basis for freedom, and the American experiment came to be seen as a struggle of cosmic proportions. America, James Madison—the framer of the Constitution—said, has become a "workshop of liberty to the civilized world," or, as Thomas Paine put it: "We have it in our power to begin the world over again."

In addition to showing moral rectitude and responsibility, the ownership of property was seen as essential to the view of freedom as personal autonomy. In this case, one of government's duties was indeed to help people gain property. This was eventually to lead to the massive expansion of the original country towards the west and the south. All of us have seen the cowboy movies and noticed the importance of this right to property. The fact that so much was taken from the Native Americans and the Mexicans was, of course, in accordance with this view of the unique mission of the Anglo-American world. The Indians, after all, were pagans, and the Mexicans were Catholics, which in that mentality was exactly the same.

Even the so-called "Bill of Rights" in the Constitution, so crucial in the future dominance of the view of freedom as personal rights, was initially inspired by the priority of economic freedom, since initially it did not apply to the states, but to the federal government only. Its purpose was to protect the property owners from a concentrated source of power. The format of the constitutional clauses shows this. They say: "Congress shall not" do this or that.

America's famous religious freedom did not originally arise out of any theory or philosophy of religious toleration, but as a consequence of the view of freedom as "self-possession." This view implies the individual liberty of conscience, which was consistent with the religious pluralism of the country at its beginning. Moreover, a multiplicity of religious convictions and communities prevented the much-feared concentration of power, just as the multiplicity of interests was seen as advantageous to civil freedom based on the possession of property. This is another reason why Catholicism and its claims to universality were so feared.

If this panorama describes the framework of the beginnings of the American debate on freedom, what initial forces propelled its expansion to include and strengthen other dimensions of freedom? I would say they were these: the challenge of slavery, the expansion to the west, the arrival of immigrants from beyond the Anglo-Saxon world, especially Catholic immigrants from Ireland, Italy, and Eastern Europe, the economic changes brought about by the Industrial Revolution, the increasingly militant movement for women's rights, as well as, of course, world events that had an impact on American global commerce. Each of these contributed to the development of the idea of freedom in America, and it is not difficult to imagine how they affected or challenged the existing dominant view.

Among these, of course, the most traumatic has been the challenge posed by the struggle for freedom of African Americans. This has been the paradigm for all the other attempts to introduce new dimensions of the ideal of freedom, and it is still so today. Today too, the lack of the particular form of freedom pursued is seen as a form of "slavery." From the continuing insistence on economic freedom to the freedoms sought by the feminist and gay political movements, the alternative is still some form of slavery. So it was for the labor movement, as seen in the use of the term "wage slavery" to refer to economic dependence as incompatible with freedom. Early feminists too referred to the "slavery of sex," including from the beginning a view of marriage itself as a potential form of slavery.

Again, when the American Revolution appealed to these initial ideas about freedom to justify itself, it essentially led to the invention of a new country based not on a cultural or ethnic or regional tradition, but on an ideal—a human ideal, which is, as I suggested above, intrinsically conflictive—that is, capable of conflicting expressions. Indeed, this process of conflict or competition itself became, paradoxically, the unifying force of this new, invented country, a "republic of the mind," as Rousseau called it.

This is really quite an amazing thing; many of America's successes, as well as its failures, are due to it. So far this is still the case, and we cannot understand American life, American politics, American religion, and American foreign policy without keeping this in mind. This conflict in the pursuit of an ideal must be fueled and sustained by hope—by hope in the country's strength to sustain the challenge of expanding and defending freedom, hope in the so-called "American dream," even if this dream in the concrete means something different for different citizens, confidence in the basic fairness of the "rules of the game," but above all, confidence in the possibility of the ideal of freedom itself.

And this is where the problem lies today. By and large the division between American conservatives and liberals has not been based on dogmatic, philosophical differences. As I have said, the American debate about freedom has never really been fueled by philosophical systems (which are generally not open to the idea of compromise as a way of sustaining debate). It has instead been defined by concrete situations, concrete challenges to the foundational framework, cast, even in its secular form, by the ethos of Protestant theology. This idea of freedom as an essentially contested concept prevents ideological dominance, and so American conservatives and liberals have both generally accepted the terms of the debate. Their difference is found mostly in their particular "interests." In admittedly too general terms, it could be said that conservatives tend to support the ideal of protecting economic freedom, whereas liberals make theirs the cause of those persons excluded by a too rigid interpretation of those same protections.

In *The Peasant of the Garonne* Jacques Maritain wrote to protest the accusation by conservatives that he had contributed to the theological and philosophical confusion and division in the Church following the Second Vatican Council. He said that liberalism and conservativism were attitudes of the heart that one seems to have been born into, so to speak, or at least were the result of experiences beyond rational analysis. Our duty, he explained, is to understand what we are like in the heart and then train our minds to think in the opposite direction.

This reminds me of Luigi Giussani's insistence that emotions are not in and of themselves obstacles to the perception of reality. On the contrary, reason that lacks affectivity is rationalism, an abstraction, an ideology. We ought to judge the emotions by considering all the dimensions of an experience, returning again and again to the fundamental or primordial exigencies of the human heart. We must keep our eyes fully open, so to speak, remain really attentive. This requires a devotion to reality, a passion for the human reality and its implications, a confidence in humanity, a determination not to exclude any of the factors involved in the quest for freedom.

This, I fear, is what is in danger today.

My friends in New York feel this, worry about it, worry about becoming cynics in order to avoid the intolerance of the rigid positions they see on both sides of the political spectrum. But cynicism is the recourse of those who have become fearful of reality, who fear that reality cannot fulfill the primordial desires of the heart which thirst always for more and more—thirst, indeed, for infinity. And this, precisely, is the problem: infinity, eternity, mystery, the religious sense. My friends are aware of this; that is really why I have been invited to be with them.

There is a problem, though, with the implications of allowing the religious dimension to enter into the contest provoked by the thirst for freedom. The problem is that modernity, as ideology, sought to cut the quest for freedom off from the link to infinity, the link to mystery. It did so in the name of freedom itself, and thus made of the quest a vicious circle from which there is no escape. I firmly believe this: once the religious sense is removed from the quest for freedom, there is absolutely no escape from the vicious circle that ensues, since human freedom is precisely a link with the infinite. That is why it cannot be defined by any ideology or closed philosophical system. It can only be pursued when reason is attentive to the religious sense.

Because my friends have not escaped the ideological prejudice of modernity against the religious sense, they can see what is needed to spark again a devotion to the quest for freedom as an ever-expanding reality but cannot imagine how it is compatible with freedom itself. And so, their "religious interest" becomes a superficial, moralizing sentimentality. Which brings us, once again, to the temptation to embrace ideological moderation. Give me moderation or give me death!

Recently, my friends and I were watching a BBC television interview with a famous terminally ill British writer who, with just a few weeks to live, desperately wished to have time to finish his last work—his "memorial," as he called it. During the interview, this remarkable man was drinking liquid morphine to calm his pain. Everyone was astounded at this passion for his work in spite of his terminal condition. This is all he asked of life, since he faced his death with remarkable serenity, willing to abandon himself to the fate that awaited him—an unknown fate, since he did not adhere to any concrete religious faith. In fact, he died only two weeks after the interview, but happily: he was indeed able to finish his work.

After viewing the video, we began to discuss it. Everyone in one way or another claimed to be terribly moved and inspired by the way this man faced his death and praised him for his heroic devotion to his work. This man showed the greatness of the human spirit, they said. A young college student present said that when she had seen the interview for the first time, she had been terrified of the implications of death, but now she had achieved a greater spiritual maturity and considered the interview greatly inspiring. An Anglican bishop—yes, there was one of them present in the discussion too, or else he was hired to portray the part in order to assure a successful soirée—spewed out all kinds of religious and spiritual platitudes about life and death.

The hostess then asked me what I thought, and of course, everyone was waiting for the opinion of this physically impressive monsignor with a funny Latin name who represented, of all things, the Catholic Church. I, of course, felt like a cockroach in a congress of hens. I decided to take seriously my own advice: listen to your heart; do not ignore anything; be attentive to reality. And so I told them, to their amazement, that I was in fact very sad, very depressed by what I saw. They asked: "How could it be?" This man's attitude to life and death was inspiring, heroic, an example to us all of spiritual maturity, they insisted. I said: "Well, maybe, but in the end he's dead. He's gone. I am sad at that. I am depressed that for all this spiritual strength and heroism, he's gone. I will never be able to meet this man. I miss him."

How could I say that, they wondered, as a religious person who believes in life after death, in God, in the spiritual? I just kept insisting that, in spite of all of that, I thought his death was sad, that it was a tragedy, that such concepts as life after death and the spirit and even God could not take away the fact that this particular interesting, fascinating, unique, and unrepeatable man was dead, that I could no longer meet him as he was in this life, in that interview. I am not satisfied with the survival of the human spirit or of particular spirits since I and my friends are obviously not just spirits. I miss his face, the sound of his voice, his gestures, his delightful British accent, his command of words, his literary creativity.

There were only two people present who sympathized with me immediately. One of them was a famous photographer, who had actually photographed this man and became his friend. He too said that he missed him. Immediately I was attracted to this man. I wanted to be his friend because he was a link to the man who had died. A photographer, I thought, must be fascinated by the concrete and the unique, and this allowed him to understand what I was trying to say. The other one was an Italian woman, a gourmet cook. Her Italian blood and love for food had not allowed her to ascend into the realms of the vague, the general, the inspiring, the abstract.

Finally, in order to give my remarks some semblance of intellectual respectability, I referred them to Dostoevsky's words in *The Brothers Karamazov* (which I stole from Giussani's book on the religious sense) where in response to possible consolations about suffering and death, it says:

> I must have retribution, or I shall destroy myself. And retribution not somewhere in the infinity of space and time, but here on earth, and so that I could see it myself. I was a believer, and I want to see for myself. And if I'm dead by that time, let them resurrect me, for if it all happens without me, it will be too unfair. Surely the reason for my suffering was not that I as well as my evil deeds and sufferings may serve as manure for some future harmony for someone else. I want to see with my own eyes the lion lie down with the lamb and the murdered man rise up and embrace his murderer. I want to be there when everyone suddenly finds out what it has all been for.

Why settle for less? Why this fear of facing what the heart really wants? This is nothing but ideological moderation, the ideology not of liberals or conservatives, but of cowards—or those who have been hurt by hoping too much.

And this is indeed the problem. Modernity abandoned the religious sense and now post-modernity tells us that we cannot hope too much. Modernity, it has been said, not only rejected belief, but has also eaten away the very disposition to believe—that is, to hope that reality corresponds to the deepest desires of the heart.

I believe that what we are facing in the United States is the inability of the Protestant framework for freedom to deal with this challenge of modernity. Classical Protestantism cannot counter modernity because, in its opposition of faith and reason, it must reject the idea of the religious sense. Indeed, in so many ways, the ideology of modernity is a child of Protestantism (which is itself the result of a distorted Catholic theology about the relation between the divine and the human). The ideology of modernity is a reaction against this view of the Christian faith. And indeed, without an appeal to reason, faith *is* an intolerant force supported by cultural and institutional power that is closed to the experience of freedom as a "contested reality."

Protestantism can only go so far in providing this framework for the contestation. At a certain point it breaks down in front of the questions posed by modernity, not to mention America's incredible pluralism and multi-culturalism, as well as its technologically-based instant involvement with the rest of the world. The original Protestant framework, then, has nothing else with which to defend itself but a moralism founded on blind faith or sentimentality. Woe to you if you do not share this faith! You will appear—as Catholicism did from the beginning—as a threat to the American dream. But then how can one remain tolerant of the new and the different? There seems to be only one way out: ideological moderation.

Because the American debate about freedom has been rooted in concrete circumstances rather than abstract philosophical conflicts, the United States has been spared the ideological warfare that has crippled this quest in other places. It therefore has an opportunity to reject the new, paralyzing ideology of moderation and continue its dedication to the quest for freedom, no longer afraid of the initial cry: Give me liberty or give me death! These are really the only two possibilities for human beings, for someone faithful to the human drama in all its implications. What I hope to bring to my friends in New York is not consolation or inspiration. I hope to urge them not to silence their hearts, not to be afraid to hope too much, not to be afraid of the thirst for infinity that is open to an immense pluralism of expressions. "Follow it," I want to tell them. "Follow it to the end!"

And then I hope to do what the apostles were doing in Solomon's Portico: to give witness to the presence of the one man in whom liberty itself conquered death.

The American Anomaly in a Secular Age

THE HISTORY OF THE UNITED STATES as a nation is inseparable from the history of the Christian faith. Whether that leads one to say that the U.S. is a "Christian nation" or not is another question. But certainly part of the reality that formed and launched the history of this nation is the Christian faith. You can see this not only in the devotion to the hundreds of American Jesuses that are found all over the landscape, but also in the terms of how the nation conceives its mission and its purpose, in the devotion to freedom and the pursuit of happiness. A cartoon in *The New Yorker* awhile back tells it all. It shows the Pilgrims coming to America, as one of them tells another, "Yes, I am going for religious freedom, but I also hope to get involved in real estate."

But is America ceasing to be influenced by the history of Christianity? I propose to you that it is not, because that which many Christians consider a threat to the Christian roots and faith of America is itself a creation of Christianity. That is to say, our secularism, relativism, and nihilism all emerge directly out of Christian claims.

I recently came across a book that illuminated these issues. In *Without Roots: The West, Relativism, Christianity, Islam*, Joseph Cardinal Ratzinger and Marcello Pera—the president of the Italian Senate and an atheist—grapple with the particular form of secularism in Europe. Pera wonders whether Europe could not do what the United States has done, that is, create some kind of non-denominational civic religion that has common values, common ways of looking at life, and common priorities. To this, Ratzinger replies:

> The unstable and fragmentary system of rules on which, to outward appearance, this [American] democracy is founded

functioned because of the thriving Protestant-Christian faith, the Protestant-Christian inspired combination of religious and moral convictions in American society. No one had prescribed or defined these convictions, but everyone assumed them as the obvious spiritual foundations. The recognition of this basic religious and moral orientation, which went beyond the single denominations and defined the society from within, reinforced the corpus of the law. . . .

In the United States, too, secularization is proceeding at an accelerated pace, and the confluence of many different cultures disrupts this basic Christian consensus. However, there is a much clearer and more implicit sense in America than in Europe that the religious and moral foundation bequeathed by Christianity is greater than that of any single denomination. Europe, unlike America, is on a collision course with its own history.

Ratzinger acknowledges that although the process of secularization is taking place here in the United States, it is happening at a slower pace than in Europe. So, the question arises: Why is this so? Why is Europe, which has such an ancient Christian tradition, unable to acknowledge that reality in the preparation of its European constitution? Why cannot it create a spiritual and moral consensus irrespective of membership in a specific faith community that will give public value to the fundamental concepts of Christianity?

Ratzinger says the historical basis of the situation can be understood this way:

American society was built for the most part by groups that had fled from the system of state churches in Europe, and they found their religious bearings in free faith communities outside of the state church. The foundations of American society were thus laid by the free churches.

I would like to expand on this point from a more precise theological perspective. When I speak of secularism or rationalism, I mean to indicate an account of reality without reference to a transcendent dimension, one which accepts the method of the sciences as the only method of inquiry into reality and maintains relativism with regard to other approaches to knowledge. Ratzinger claims that in the United States the secularizing process is occurring, but at a slower pace than in Europe. And this has to do with the very origins of American

Christianity in the so-called "free church" experience, a grassroots experience of Christian faith that is not tied to power.

But I further maintain that the process of secularization itself is logical, given a certain distortion or derailment of Christianity. This rationalism or secularism is itself a decayed form of the Christian faith. It is engendered by a Christian faith that has lost something.

In order to make this point, I would like to summarize Father Luigi Giussani's five "withouts," five developments that occurred in the experience of the Church—within the Christian experience itself—that lead to this present situation of rationalism and secularism (from his book *L'uomo e il suo destino*).

The claim is that secularism is the fruit of something that happened to Christian experience. So in that sense, is America a Christian nation? If by Christian nation we mean a nation that has been affected by what happened to the Christian faith, then America certainly fulfills the criterion, and not only in its origin in the Protestant Christianity of the free churches, but also in its post-Christian trajectory. In the end, if America becomes finally and fully secularized, that secularization would be a product of Christianity itself.

The first without: *God without Christ.* A fundamental Christian claim is "God through Christ." God is known, grasped, only because in Jesus Christ this otherwise ungraspable mystery became a tangible, visible, concrete human reality so that we have an experience of this mystery in and through human experience. Indeed, many of the efforts of the Catholic Church from the Second Vatican Council until today are attempts to revive this experience among Catholics. It is the Second Vatican Council's Pastoral Constitution on the Church in the Modern World, *Gaudium et Spes*, that gave Pope John Paul II the line that became practically the banner of almost everything he wrote: "Christ, the final Adam, by the revelation of the mystery of the Father and his love, fully reveals man to man himself and makes his supreme calling clear" (*Gaudium et Spes*, 22).

In other words, only in the mystery of Christ is the mystery of what it means to be human fully disclosed. And at the Council's end, Paul VI proclaimed that the Church was prepared to show Christianity as a human experience—that is to say, an experience of what it means to be human. The original problem, then, from the perspective of Catholic theology, has to do with this relation between God and

Christ. This is the original break, the detachment from which everything else follows. It is a loss of what the Incarnation means. After all, Christianity stands or falls with the doctrine of the Incarnation of the mystery, God becoming flesh—that is, an earthly, human reality.

Once this break occurs, it leads to the second without: *the experience of Christ without the Church*. The separation between Christ and God leads to the separation between Christ and the Church. As a result, Jesus Christ becomes a figure that is no longer contemporary to us. He becomes a figure from the past—or from above, if you wish—to be known by some kind of spirit-induced vision or conviction. After this happens, there is no longer any way to verify the Christian faith; Christ has slipped beyond the experience of life in this world. There is no way to verify the contemporaneity of Christ or to have the Christian encounter with a reality that is present today as much as it was two thousand years ago. We can believe it or feel it or become inspired by it, but there is no evidence for us in this world. The Church offered itself as evidence, a place to which one could turn to arrive at a conclusion, yes or no, with regard to Christ. Looking at the Church was looking at contemporary evidence for Christ. Once Christ is separated from the Church, then there is no evidence in this world that we can use to verify the Christian claims.

What happens to the Church when this happens is the third without: the Church loses the experience of its presence in the world, as a reality of the world. *The Church without the world*. God without Christ, Christ without Church, Church without world. When Christ has been removed from the Church, the Church is no longer useful for verifying the claims of Christianity. It exists henceforth only by two powers.

One is a kind of *spiritualism*: faith detached from experience, privatized into some kind of interior, emotional experience, a sentimentalization of the faith. When a doctrine like the resurrection, with its implications of what it means to live in this world, has no way of being verified, what power does it have? What remains is only the interior power it can exercise in one's spiritual life.

The opposite possibility, but having the same origin, is *clericalism*. The Church sustains itself by codifying itself in a kind of literary fundamentalism or legalism or moralism. It is the emergence of a power that calls the shots, that interprets what is or is not compatible with a Christian faith that can no longer be verified.

Neither kind of Church can be a protagonist in history—neither can generate a culture. The Church becomes what Giussani calls a "courtesan" of cultural, political, and social history. Where real life takes place, the Church just goes along, trying to hang in there and make sure it doesn't disappear merely through the influence it can exercise.

The fourth without: once God and Christ have been separated, Christ has been spiritualized away and the Church has been privatized away, the world is deprived of the sense of personhood. The fourth "without" is *the world without "I."* Perhaps the step from three to four is the most difficult one to grasp. But it is evident in our historical development. The sense of the uniqueness and unrepeatability of the person—and how this is lived in concrete relationships—is lost, or at least weakened. To the degree that the sense of personhood is weakened, one is exposed to all kinds of manipulations by power. A power external to us rules, leading to a kind of internal alienation, to our construction of little, self-defensive worlds.

Finally, living in a world without "I" leads to the fifth without: *the "I" without God*—that is to say, radical secularism, the loss of hope and trust in the goodness of reality and of life. But the need for religion remains, and so it creates all kinds of pantheistic spiritualizations designed to ease the burden of being a person. A kind of not-caring emerges. "Why should I care about the pursuit of happiness? Why should I want to be free? Why not just settle for what we can?" The fourth and fifth "withouts" describe the situation we already have in some places and the possible future in others. But they all come from the first split, the separation of God and Christ. They all come from a culture that was generated by belief in an Incarnation and then suddenly or gradually lost that conviction.

Relativism and secularism are consequences of the dis-incarnation of the mystery. This is not a return to pre-Christianity. It is post-Christianity—because it rejects what is claimed to have taken place.

As a summary of this process, I propose this: At the heart of this dramatic situation is the separation between faith and life. What the Christian faith proclaims is no longer experienced as corresponding to real life. Real life is that life that can fulfill those desires of the heart that move us and animate us; it is what supports us and sustains us.

The loss of that experience has led to the loss of the Christian proposal about life. This lack of correspondence between the way the faith is proposed and lived and life as it is experienced certainly dis-incarnates Christ, removes him from this world into a non-verifiable other world. God, who remains an enigma, the reason for which one might want to live, becomes totally invisible, totally ungraspable. One quickly gets tired of that ungraspable enigma and chooses something lower to worship, creating idolatry, which in its modern form is the same as ideology. Where faith and experience in life are united, this process is prevented from continuing, or it is, at the very least, slowed down.

I believe this way of looking at things coincides with what Ratzinger says about the importance for American history of the dominant Christian faith of the free church—the grassroots, independent faith community. In these free churches, faith was not separated from life. Faith was an experience. It was more linked to life than in the official state churches of Europe. You can see this in the public role the free churches play, in their demand for protection and recognition. The American separation of church and state had a motivation and configuration that could not be more different from the conflictual expression of church and state imposed by the French Revolution and the systems that followed it. As Ratzinger puts it:

> In America the state is little more than a free space for different religious communities to congregate; it is in its nature to recognize and permit these communities to exist in their particularity and their non-membership in the state. This is a separation conceived positively, since it is meant to allow religion to be itself, a religion that respects and protects its own living space distinctly from the state and its ordinances. This separation has created a special relationship between the state and the private spheres that is completely different from Europe. The private sphere has an absolutely public character.

Faith has a public character because it has not been separated from life. As long as this can last, the descent into radical relativism or secularism can be halted or slowed down. However, when the reality of the Church disappears, it becomes impossible to sustain this union between faith and life, as we have seen.

And so, the second "without" must be prevented, Christ without the Church. And this is the weak point in the American resistance to secularism. Given the Protestant nature of the dominant Christianity, the experience of the Church, the life of the Church, is weakened, and thus the way is paved for the third "without," the Church without the world. The key is not to separate faith from the experience of belonging to that communion called the Church. It is that reality that concretizes the presence of Christ as a fact, as an event that can and must be verified precisely by its correspondence to the needs of the human heart. The experiences of the free churches and the Protestantism it generated cannot sustain the advance toward secularism, rationalism, and nihilism forever. It cannot prevent this dissolution of Protestant Christianity into the culture, as has already happened in mainstream Protestantism. Evangelicals who still have this experience of faith and life will not be able, by themselves, to halt this process because of their lack of experience of the Church.

It is, therefore, a moment of question for the Catholic Church. The process of dissolution began within the Catholic Church. The Second Vatican Council made every effort to reverse this course. John Paul II made it his task to provoke within the Catholic Church an awakening of the relation between faith and life and the Church, a task that leads to an invitation to non-believers precisely because faith, in not being separated from life, is not separated from reason—and reason is what we have in common.

The fact that we have a book co-authored by an atheist and by the man who became Pope Benedict XVI shows what is possible. If the Christian, like Pope Benedict, feels no opposition between faith and life, it is possible to meet the very children the Church has created in the ground of reason. Faith, the Pope says, helps us guide and purify our reason, and then within it we can approach, with respect, anyone. And this, and only this, can create a consensus that will generate a new culture.

Learning to Say "I"

Modernity and the Problem of Identity

IN 1996 LEON WIESELTIER, the literary editor of the influential American political and cultural weekly magazine *The New Republic*, wrote a book called *Against Identity*, a collection of seventy-four aphorisms or thoughts. These dealt with questions, objections, and reflections on how the experience of identity is lived in the United States today. Wieseltier intends to attack the obsession with identity that characterizes American politics and culture by rehabilitating the idea of individualism against communitarianism.

Wieseltier believes that today's concept of identity is contrary to the individualism that has characterized American history and that it therefore threatens the political advantages of a society built on the individual. His book is a powerful demonstration of the impossibility of finding a resolution to the clash between an experience of identity—which implies a belonging where freedom, if it exists, takes the form of acceptance of what is given—and an individualism in which freedom is the capacity to go beyond the limitations of what is given.

He writes:

> In America the tribunes of identity are the tribunes of diversity, but the joke is on them. Their ends are contradictory. Diversity means complexity. Identity means simplicity. Anybody who takes diversity seriously will see that identity is an illusion. The multiculturalists will reply that there is no contradiction, that America is a complex society of differently simplified individuals, a multicultural society of monocultural people. But they misunderstand America. The American achievement is not the multicultural society, it is the multicultural individual.

According to Wieseltier, American history has been driven by the tension between the individual and identity. The tension is resolved through the primacy of an individual who is able to belong to more than one self-defining community of belonging. "Identity is a promise of singleness," he writes, "but this is a false promise. Many things are possible in America, but the singleness of identity is not one of them." As a friend of mine observed, it is very difficult to say "I" in America.

It is moving to see how the author seeks to escape the impasse between the experience and demands of an identity defined by a belonging that excludes others and those of originality, freedom, creativity, diversity, and solidarity with "outsiders." "Identity is very social," he observes, "but it is not very sociable, for the definition of the individual that it provides is not least a negative definition. A definition not only in terms of what one is, but also in terms of what one is not, and such a definition of the same will often be experienced by the other as a rejection." In any case, he insists, "it is never the case, even with simple objects, that there is a single criterion of identity. The ascription of identity is the consequence of a choice between the criteria of identity. We have many identities, but we do not reward them all with significance."

Must we be content with this, then, with being an "I" that chooses the identity that best fits the circumstances of his life? In some circles this is considered a pathological psychological situation. In the end, having many identities is to cease being a single, free-acting, sovereign subject, a person.

This dilemma is the problem of modernity, as Wieseltier recognizes: "Identity is not to be mistaken with individuality. Individuality is ancient; identity is modern."

The problem or the clash between the experience of being a free individual and someone whose "I" is defined by belonging to a group is an expression of the drama of personhood. The person is incommunicable. As Thomas Aquinas recognized, each person is, in a certain way, the entire universe. At the same time, the experience of personhood is inseparable from the experience of a need for another, the experience that Pope John Paul II called "original solitude": an "I" awakened by the need of a "you." This is the drama of personal existence.

This problem is the consequence of the "polarity" or tension that defines human existence. Wieseltier quotes Marcel Mauss: "It is plain that there has never existed a human being who has not been aware, not only of his body, but at the same time, of his individuality, both spiritual and physical." In the same vein, Hans Urs von Balthasar describes the polarities that are expressive of the dramatic nature of human existence: spirit/body, male/female, and individual/community. These three polarities are inseparable, and they are expressions of a deeper mystery. They point to the link between each human person and the infinite mystery that is our origin and our destiny. Human life consists precisely in seeking to live these polarities without destroying the uniqueness and un-repeatability of the person. Moreover, the "solution" to the problem necessarily involves freedom. It is this that makes life a drama.

I would like to propose that the problem of identity as experienced today is the result of the inability of modernity to deal with all the dimensions of the drama of personhood. Wieseltier himself observes: "Individuality is ancient, identity is modern. . . . It is more plausible to think of identity as the solution to the problem of individuality."

What do we mean by modernity? Here I am not entering the debate about the nature of modernity, post-modernity, and so on. I want to reflect on this topic from a theological perspective, that is, from the perspective of faith and the "purification of reason" (Pope Benedict XVI) that faith provides. Rather than enter into a philosophical debate, I appeal to the daily experience of life in societies that see themselves as modern, as progressive, as liberal. I have in mind what the political and cultural critic Paul Berman, in the provocative book *Terror and Liberalism*, calls "liberalism." This is how Berman describes the dominant mentality in modern society:

> What was the secret behind those many areas of progress, the all-powerful, all-conquering principle?
>
> It was the recognition that all of life is not governed by a single all-knowing and all-powerful authority—by a divine force. It was the tolerant idea that every sphere of human activity—science, technology, politics, religion, and private life—should operate independently of the others, without trying to yoke everything together under a single guiding hand. It was belief in the many, instead of the one. It was an insistence on freedom of thought and freedom of action—not on absolute freedom, but on something truer, stronger, and more reliable than absolute freedom, which is relative freedom: a

freedom that recognizes the existence of other freedoms, too. Freedom consciously arrived at. Freedom that is chosen, and not just bestowed by God on high. This idea was, in the broadest sense, liberalism—liberalism not as a rigid doctrine but as a state of mind, a way of thinking about life and reality.

This way of thinking may have been abandoned by post-modern thinkers in universities, but it is still the dominant thinking of most people in modern, democratic societies. Indeed, Berman shows how World War I destroyed for many this dream of liberalism and created the conditions for the violent totalitarianism that was to follow, leading all the way to modern terrorism. Still, unless the present threat of terrorism changes the mentality, when most people think of a modern, progressive society, they dream about this liberalism.

As Berman recognizes, the basis for this way of thinking is the denial that the human heart is made, structured, or given as a yearning for a mystery that man is unable to reach. Indeed, at the root of modernity is the cutting short of what Giussani called the religious sense. The problem of identity, Wieseltier acknowledges, originates in this demand for totality. "The lure of identity," he writes, "is the lure of wholeness. It proposes to bind up the parts and the pieces of a life and transform them into a unity, into a life that adds up." ("Adds up" means that it makes sense when related to a totality.) "This provides a mixture of psychological and aesthetic elation. But is there really nothing worse than a life that does not add up?"

Yes there is, believes Wieseltier: the life that does add up is worse. It is a paralyzing, easy life. "The thirst for wholeness is indistinguishable from the thirst for death. Only religion is candid enough to say so," he writes.

Therefore, the alleviation, if not the solution, of the problem of identity and individuality seems to require the cutting short of the desire for wholeness, of the religious sense.

But this begs a question: if this mystery is forever unreachable, if it is always hopelessly beyond all our efforts to reach it, why fear an encounter with it? In reality, the mystery as an ineffable, unreachable, infinite, unimaginable reality poses no problem to the experience of an "open-ended" individuality. In this case, the on-going quest for satisfaction of the desires of the heart would propel the human adventure as this satisfaction is freely pursued all the way to infinity, so to speak.

If the religious sense is only the experience of an opening to infinity, it poses no threat to individuality.

The feared clash is not with the mystery as such. What is feared is a revelation of the mystery. What is feared is an incarnation of the mystery. This is the fear that has created modernity and its inability to deal with the drama of personhood, the impasse between identity, belonging, community, and freedom.

This is my proposal: the modern problem of individuality versus an identity defined by belonging is the result of modernity's fear of the possibility of an Incarnation.

Indeed, the drama of modernity—the "drama of atheist human-ism," as Henri De Lubac called it—is the drama of reason. It was in the name of reason as opposed to superstition that modernity offered its advantages to humankind. But the culmination of reason's pursuit of meaning, which coincides with the heart's pursuit of happiness and sustains the experience of being an "I," is not simply the recognition of the mystery's utter transcendence. This would make of human life a tragedy. Such a situation would indeed tempt reason to rebel against its own dynamism and settle for less than full satisfaction, or to iden-tify the partial with the total, as in the various forms of idolatry, or to embrace a destructive nihilism. Reason's quest is much more than that.

As Alberto Savorana puts it: "The fruit of the rationalistic men-tality is the fact that today we can find those who, using reason, come to admit mystery, but very few for whom the apex of reason is the presentiment that the Mystery intercepts my humanity, very few for whom reason is at the height of its exercise when it registers something that happens. . . . The true drama of man is not whether to believe in God or not. In this context, Father Giussani said that the great dogma of modernity is the impossibility of revelation."

"The impossibility of revelation"—this is the key to understand-ing modernity's failure to reconcile individualism and identity based on the experience of belonging. The dogma of the impossibility of revelation forces modernity to give up on the possibility of grasping the reason for the polarities that define human existence and therefore prevents us from grasping what it means to be a person.

Because of its basis in the rejection of reason's presentiment of revelation, there is no true modernity until the appearance of a claim that revelation had taken place—more so, that the Incarnation has actually taken place. Modernity therefore is truly a post-Christian phenomenon. It is the consequence of the "dis-Incarnation" of Christ.

Protestantism led a great portion of Christianity to the denial of reason's ability to have a presentiment of revelation because of its view of nature and grace. It is no surprise that modernity made its appearance in cultures heavily influenced by Protestant moralism. But, in spite of the role of Protestantism in giving rise to modernity, its true origins lie within the Catholic Church, as a corrupt form of Catholicism.

T.S. Eliot posed the question: has mankind abandoned the Church or has the Church abandoned mankind? Luigi Giussani replied: both. In the rise of the ideologies of modernity, mankind abandoned the Church. But the Church abandoned mankind when it was embarrassed by Christ, when Christianity ceased being presented as an event and faith as beginning with a human encounter. This diminished Catholicism led to an intellectual and moral system in which it was difficult to find a role for the Incarnation except as a way to pay for the damage of sin. Indeed, Catholic theologians were able to imagine a destiny of perfect happiness—the natural end of man—achieved without sharing the life of Christ. Modernity is the child of this terrible mistake.

This is precisely why when the Church decided to engage in a dialogue with modernity, the Second Vatican Council sought to repair the damage by its famous declaration of *Gaudium et Spes*, 22: the mystery of man cannot be fully grasped when it is separated from the mystery of Christ. Christ's revelation of the mystery of the Father and his love (the mystery of the Trinity) reveals man to man himself. The end, purpose, destiny of each single human person cannot be grasped without the revelation of the mystery in human flesh as the mystery of a trinitarian God. Outside of the consequences of this fact, the efforts and failures of modernity are fully understandable. The reality of the human heart and its constitutive needs—the reality of reason and the dramatic nature of its quest for meaning, for totality—cannot be separated from the mystery of Jesus Christ.

Indeed, it is by seeking to express adequately its experience of the event of Christ that the Church contributed to civilization the notion of the person as a unique and unrepeatable subject. Recall the Decree of the Council of Chalcedon in the year 451:

Our Lord Jesus Christ [is] the same perfect in divinity and perfect in humanity, the same truly God and truly man, of a rational soul and a body; consubstantial with the Father as regards his divinity, and the same consubstantial with us as regards his humanity; like us in all respects except for sin; begotten before the ages from the Father as regards his divinity, and in the last days the same for us and for our salvation from Mary, the virgin God-bearer as regards his humanity; one and the same Christ, Son, Lord, only-begotten, acknowledged in two natures which undergo no confusion, no change, no division, no separation; at no point was the difference between the natures taken away through the union, but rather the property of both natures is preserved and comes together into a single person and a single subsistent being; he is not parted or divided into two persons, but is one and the same only-begotten Son, God, Word, Lord Jesus Christ, just as the prophets taught from the beginning about him, and as the Lord Jesus Christ himself instructed us, and as the creed of the fathers handed it down to us.

The achievement of America might be the multicultural individual at the cost of the full experience of belonging (and maybe this is the best solution modernity can offer), but the achievement of the Church is the recognition of the individual human person who, in sharing the life of Christ, is united to the mystery without the loss of any of his constitutive dimensions of existence. Individual and community, freedom and belonging, body and soul—all are held together with "no confusion, no change, no division, no separation." Reason and freedom need not fear this manifestation of the Mystery, for in Christ the human and divine natures do not clash, "but rather the property of both natures is preserved and comes together into a single person and a single subsistent being; he is not parted or divided into two persons, but is one and the same only-begotten Son, God, Word, Lord Jesus Christ."

Indeed, the polarities themselves exist because each human being was created to share the life of Jesus Christ. Because he reveals the mystery to be a trinitarian communion of absolute love, a share in his life is the only destiny that can satisfy the desires of the human heart.

It is not surprising that in the places where the mystery of Christ is not known or accepted, human life becomes a tragedy to be made bearable by the contradictions, reductions, and suppressions of a modernity trying desperately to preserve the fruits of the Incarnation while rejecting the event itself. Such an arrangement cannot last; it leads ultimately to nihilism.

Before the publication of Pope Benedict XVI's first encyclical, *Deus Caritas Est*, many expected Benedict to condemn the destructive consequences of the errors of modernity's relativism. Certainly Benedict was aware of the deepest origins of modern relativism and the tragic results of its attempt to protect freedom by the curtailment of the scope of reason and suppression of the heart's attraction to infinity. The problem, he recognized, originates in the denial of both the possibility and reality of the Incarnation. For this reason, he turned to the first Epistle of John, where the author is struggling against the denial of the truth about Christ in his community. It is in this letter that we find the declaration that *Deus caritas est*, "God is love" (1 Jn 4:16).

"God is love" is not a theological or philosophical statement for the author of 1 John. It is what Father Giussani would call a judgment: the conclusion of a process of judging reality. It is a judgment made possible because of the experience of belonging to the companionship created by the Incarnation. The reality of this unity is what makes possible the judgment that God is love. Nor is the judgment "God is love" based on an emotional experience. "We have come to know and to believe in the love God has for us" (1 Jn 4:16), the author writes, not because of an emotion, but because of a fact, an event.

A judgment is the result of a process, a path, an itinerary. This path is called education. The judgment "God is love" is the fruit of an education of the human heart, what 1 John calls "love brought to perfection" (1 Jn 4:17). The author of the epistle is not just condemning those in the community who denied the Incarnation. He is inviting us to enter into the logic of love, to follow the educational itinerary of the love that has its origins in God.

The one who loves, he says, reveals his identity as someone who is begotten by God. It is indeed a matter of "identity," that is, of the "I." A new "I" is generated through the education of the heart in love, a new identity which is very different from a "multicultural individual." This new "I" is a new identity created by love, and united to others by love.

"Everyone who loves," says 1 John, "knows God" (1 Jn 4:7). Knows in what sense? Biblically, to "know" something means to have experienced it. The one who loves has experienced that God is love, experienced it because God has revealed his love.

The love in us is a revelation of a relationship that God has established with us. It is not we who have built the bridge to God, we who have loved God first. Rather, *he* has first loved us. I cannot say, "Love leads me to God." But I can say, "God comes to me because God is love."

In the end, the conclusion *Deus est caritas* is not just some kind of religious sentiment or a philosophical intuition of the nature of God. It is the description of the judgment made by those living within this companionship who share Christ's life. It is this bond, this friendship, this unity, that awakens in me this awareness. If I have experienced this communion, then I can say, "God is love."

"God is love" is a Johannine formula linked to two others that are similar. Another one is "God is light" (1 Jn 1:5). It indicates the experience of not seeing and then seeing, of not recognizing and then recognizing—above all of not knowing, and now knowing. This declaration refers to the effect of the Incarnation on human reason. The "education of the human heart in love" is also the "education of reason," or as Benedict calls it, the "purification of reason." This is the point at which faith intersects the human efforts to build a just and free society, one in which the revelation of love reconciles identity with individuality.

Another consequence of faith in the Incarnation, of the encounter with Christ, is what Jesus says to Nicodemus and to the Samaritan woman: "God is spirit" (Jn 4:24). This judgment comes from the experience of a power that is greater than the power of our efforts to reach the fulfillment of our human possibilities. "God is spirit" expresses the experience that this fulfillment is indeed possible, giving rise to a hope that moves us to commit our freedom to offer witness in this world, to the possibility of a fulfillment that the world cannot give.

1 John is also where we find this statement: "We are God's children now; what we shall be has not yet been revealed. We do know that when it is revealed we shall be like him, for we shall see him as he is" (1 Jn 3:2). From the perspective of the Incarnation, to live "in Christ" means to be already a child of God, generated by God, even as we do not know its full meaning. That is, I do not know what I am already, who I am already. Belonging to the "body of Christ," being a person in Christ, does not give us an identity closed into itself. Rather, it gives us the experience of an identity in this world that is experienced, so to

speak, in formation, in gestation. It is an identity experienced as being continually born again, as Scripture itself claims, through *metanoia* or conversion.

An obstacle to this understanding is the Protestant reduction of these terms to the moral dimension, the first step in the direction of their modern interpretation in psychological terms. To get beyond that obstacle we must be as bold as Pope Benedict XVI, who compared the risen state of Christ's body to an evolutionary jump in the constitution of the human being and portrayed the resurrection's effect on Christ's humanity as the completion of the creation of the human being. The Catholic doctrine of the Assumption of Mary also marks an important growth in our understanding of personhood according to the Incarnation. The reality of the Eucharist incorporating us into the Body of Christ as a communion of life is another vital part of this vision of the identity of the human person and its destiny.

The identity of the person of Christ cannot be exhausted by the present forms of his or her belonging in terms of race, ethnicity, gender, nationhood, etc. Still, nothing that is of value as a demonstration of the fruitfulness of God's creative love is lost when incorporated into Christ. The stronger the Christian identity, the greater the capacity for a diversity that reflects the richness of the trinitarian communion. The Christian "I" in Christ is a capacity to be possessed and transformed by trinitarian love.

The impasse between an identity constituted by a belonging and the individuality characteristic of modernity can be overcome by our faith in a way that preserves the value of the experiences that proponents of either side are attempting to preserve. In the face of this impasse, the Church's contribution to the drama of modern life is nothing more than being faithful to what she received from the Lord, that is to be faithful to herself.

III. A PASSION FOR THE INFINITE

The Mystery and the Holocaust

Reason and the Religious Sense in the Face of a "Bad Infinity"

FAITH, AND THE THEOLOGIES that originate in it, cannot claim to understand such evil as that of the Holocaust. No one can honestly go beyond what the author of the book of Job understood: all "explanations" for the reality of innocent suffering are false and must be rejected. The response of the believer must be a personal solidarity with those who suffer by suffering with them, that is, by being willing to share the existential anguish of their question—why?—and turning this anguish into a prayer for redemption.

The introduction to the first edition of Elie Wiesel's *Night*, the first book of his trilogy on the Holocaust, was written by the French Catholic author François Mauriac. As a young Israeli journalist, Wiesel had once come to interview Mauriac for a Tel Aviv newspaper. Mauriac told him that the sight of Jewish children forcibly separated from their mothers at the Austerlitz train station made him touch for the first time "that mystery of iniquity whose exposure marked the end of an era and the beginning of another."

Then Mauriac makes this observation:

> The dream conceived by Western man in the eighteenth century, whose dawn he thought he had glimpsed in 1789, and which until August 2, 1914, had become stronger with the advent of the Enlightenment and scientific discoveries—that dream finally vanished for me before those trainloads of small children. And yet I was still thousands of miles away from imagining that these children were destined to feed the gas chambers and crematoria.

Mauriac was referring to the dream about human progress and freedom based on reason set free from all religious constraints. This dream ended with the Holocaust. The rationality it proclaimed was applied to the design of ever more efficient technologies of death; the absolute subjectivism it proposed disappeared in the reduction of persons to mere samples of social, racial, or ethnic definitions; the interiority it claimed to defend was eliminated in the radical de-personalization of a society viewed as an economic or industrial apparatus at the service of ideology; the progress it promised led not to Paradise on earth, but to what has been called "a dress rehearsal for Hell."

This failure has not led to a re-consideration of the value of the religious faith from which reason sought absolute freedom. Religious faith is still considered partly responsible for creating the intolerant, absolutist way of thinking that leads to such inhuman situations. Instead, the failure of the dream of human progress based on reason has led to a rejection of reason itself as capable of grasping reality. Ambiguity has become the treasured value in our thinking and speaking.

But is this the proper response to the totalitarian ideologies which have been the plague of this century? I don't think so. On the contrary, this lack of confidence in reason paves the way for new forms of intolerance.

It is not possible to explain or to fully understand the suffering of the innocent because it belongs to the religious dimension of human life—that is, the relation between the human being and infinity. I believe the Holocaust is an expression of this mystery. In a strikingly prophetic essay written before the Holocaust, Emmanuel Levinas described what he called "Hitlerism" as an "awakening of elementary sentiments." These, he argued, "express the primordial attitude of a soul before the totality of the real and its own destiny."

This attitude or stance before the totality of reality is exactly what is meant by the religious sense. In effect, Levinas saw that the Nazi ideology originated in the religious imagination. As such, Levinas thought that Hitlerism was in conflict, not only with political liberalism, but with Christianity and, indeed, any other expression of the religious stance before reality.

The religious instinct, however, will not go away. The human heart will always thirst for certainty, for meaning, for a deeper and deeper vision into the mysteries that surround us and break upon us unexpectedly in crucial moments of life. The human heart will always reach out to infinity, and nothing which forces human beings to suppress or crush this desire can satisfy human needs. Sooner or later the need will assert itself.

This passion for infinity is the religious sense. If there is no path open so that this passion for infinity can be adequately pursued, it will construct for itself what has been called cases of "bad infinity" (these used to be called "idols"), leading to ideological intolerance and political oppression. The Holocaust is what can happen when the religious sense is separated from its orientation to the truly infinite.

Only an adequate understanding of the religious sense protects us from its idolatrous alternatives.

Such an understanding requires that reason and the religious sense not be separated. The contemporary disdain for the capacity of human reason abandons the religious sense to the irrational, thus paving the way for the worship of those idols of racial, ethnic, or national identity which led to the Holocaust and the other barbarous planned and systematic horrors so characteristic of our time.

The alternative to the rationalism of the modern dream is not the limitation of reason, but a true understanding of it as precisely the capacity to take us to the portal of that truly transcendent mystery for which the religious sense thirsts.

I am aware that religious intolerance has been a real experience for many. For this reason, religious participation in the public arena of discussion and formulation of policy and legislation is feared as the return to the dark ages. Every time some religious pathology claims its victims the assertion is made that all religious behavior tends towards this conclusion. Religion is welcomed only when it is reduced to harmless sentimentality or a socially convenient disposition to self-control. What makes us afraid is the claim of the presence in the world of the infinite mystery for which the heart desires. This fear leads many to deny the religious roots of all truly human cultures. This same fear denies the capacity of reason to recognize the presence of a transcendent mystery. The rejection of reason's openness to the mystery of God led to the end of the modern dream in the Holocaust. We can only wonder to what horror the rejection of reason itself can take us.

In his book *The Religious Sense*, Father Luigi Giussani defines reason as a "relationship with the infinite that reveals itself as the need for a total explanation. Reason's highest achievement," he writes, "is the intuition that an explanation exists exceeding the measure of reason itself." The religious sense, guided by reason, will thus reject as false all idols created by the human mind.

To be sure, the temptation to idolatry always remains. Somehow we refuse to open ourselves totally to a reality that we cannot control. Thus the derailment of reason and the corruption of the religious sense. Then, should the mystery reveal itself, it will appear as undeserved grace.

Remembering his meeting with Eli Wiesel, François Mauriac writes:

> Did I explain to him that what had been a stumbling block for *his* faith had become a cornerstone for *mine*? And that the connection between the cross and human suffering remains, in my view, the key to the unfathomable mystery in which the faith of his childhood was lost? And yet, Zion has risen up out of the crematoria and the slaughterhouses. The Jewish nation has been resurrected from among its thousands of dead. It is they who have given it new life. We do not know the worth of one single drop of blood, one single tear. All is grace. If the Almighty is the Almighty, the last word for each of us belongs to Him. This is what I should have said to the Jewish child."

But Mauriac didn't. Because the religious sense guided by reason ends at the portal of grace, Mauriac writes that instead of telling him what he had come to believe and understand through his faith, "All I could do was embrace him and weep."

This is how authentic religious faith responds to the Holocaust.

Everything is Grace

Augustine's Two Cities After 9/11

I WANT TO ADDRESS THE roots of the problem, the ultimate reasons for the mentality that prevents so many—including otherwise very good and ethical people—from recognizing the horror of abortion and other attacks against human life that are characteristic of what Pope John Paul II called the "culture of death."

The root of our problem is the mystery that Christian faith calls original sin. The root of our problem is not faulty science, or inadequate education in ethical values, or the exercise of political and economic power by perverse people, or a lack of religious fervor and beliefs, or the weak faith of believers, or the love of pleasure and riches, or any other humanly understandable cause. The origin of our problem is a mystery—a tragedy that affects us all equally, religious and non-religious, believers and non-believers, moral and immoral. The root of our problem is a tragedy from which we cannot escape by our own efforts, or politics, or education, or good examples, or religious inspirations, or social renewal.

The root of our problem is a situation from which we must be rescued by a power greater than our best intentions and attempts.

The root of a plant is what sustains it, what keeps it in place, alive and feeding from the environment. We usually do not see the roots of a plant or tree. They are hidden under the ground. In order to see them, we have to dig deep until they are fully exposed. We have to dig to the very level below which the plant is no longer there; we have to dig to the "origin" of the plant. The quest for the roots of a particular situation or problem points us to its origin, to the beginning of its existence. If we grasp this beginning, this origin, we will understand the magnitude of the problem and the challenge it poses. Using the language of Pope John Paul II, we are seeking to look at the "genetic moment" of the "culture of death."

That is why the question about the roots or origins of a human situation is a religious question. By religious I mean that it pertains to the origin, purpose, and destiny of human life. The religious sense is the human quest for the meaning of life, the quest for the big picture that serves as a measure for judging the particular meaning of what happens. Religion is identical to the desire to understand when applied to reality in all its dimensions. When allowed full sway, the religious sense will point us to a mystery that surpasses everything that can be said, imagined, or grasped. The roots of all the manifestations of the human reality are thus found within this mystery. That is why I say that the problem of ultimate roots is a religious problem. It seeks to discover the relation between this mystery and what motivates human beings in particular, the roots of the human capacity for welcoming, affirming and promoting life—or for destroying it.

Actually, this question of the origin or roots of our problem has been more or less in the minds of most Americans since the tragic events of September 11, 2001. I say "more or less" because, soon after the initial shock, all kinds of mechanisms began to reduce for us the scope of the question. When this happens, answers are announced prematurely before the question is allowed to penetrate deeper into our experience. For many, the quest for the ultimate answer stops with those partial answers. It is as if we are afraid to go to deeper levels. Perhaps some fear falling into political incorrectness by harboring thoughts that the official culture rejects.

As soon as we began to grasp what happened on September 11, it became clear that the ultimate nature of the attack against us was religious. By destroying the Twin Towers and part of the Pentagon, the terrorists did not think they were going to mortally wound American power. The targets were chosen as symbols of power. This was a symbolic gesture, so to speak, the type of statement or affirmation typical of religious behavior. The people who crashed those planes into the World Trade Center and the Pentagon saw themselves as religious martyrs. We have unavoidable proof of that in the literature left behind by one of them in the car he took to the airport, literature urging him to think of the paradise that awaited him and not to be afraid of death.

But rather than face it as such, all kinds of ways were found to avoid this issue. It was said that the terrorists were not authentically religious, that they were *using* religion to justify their hatred, or that they were just completely insane. Religious people went out of their way to insist that this kind of behavior is absolutely incompatible with any authentic religion, especially Islam, which the terrorists saw themselves as following. But that is not the issue. The issue is not why any particular religion was being used to justify the hatred that inspired such acts; the issue is the religious nature of the hatred itself. This is what many had trouble facing.

During that first week after the horror, I heard two people trying to understand the religious nature of what had happened. One was David Letterman. His show may not be the best forum for religious discussion, but again and again Letterman said he wanted to understand how it was possible to claim a religious motivation for such violence against innocent people. For a week he brought onto the show the usual parade of TV gurus of culture, and they could not answer—nor even really understand—the question. By the end of the week, Letterman had given up, and the deepest level reached was, as usual, psychological, or maybe even "philosophical," that is, the conflict between views about freedom and human rights.

The other person who publicly recognized the ultimately religious nature of the conflict was Jerry Falwell, who said the attacks were God's retribution against feminists, abortionists, and homosexuals, before he was led to claim that he had not expressed himself properly. He was right about the religious meaning of the events, however idiotic his statement was. But we must absolutely reject all suggestions of moral equivalence, as if anti-life violence were a matter of numbers or interchangeable sins. There is absolutely nothing that anyone did at any time that justifies the death of a single innocent person, not to mention 3,000. Such a suggestion is obscene.

I believe we must also reject the view that God allowed what happened on September 11 to awaken us to our culture's offenses against life and human nature. I don't know how we can say things like that and not see ourselves in the company of those theologians and religious friends of Job who tried to explain to him the reason for his sufferings. God rejected their arguments and offered Job no explanation for what had happened. Instead, he asked him questions that led Job to recognize that his true need was to be convinced that God had not rejected him, that he had not broken his covenant with his people. Anything else was beyond his power of understanding, and he was happy to recognize that God would always be a mystery beyond human comprehension. What mattered was to know that this mystery was not his enemy.

In the New Testament, Jesus also rejected a direct connection between tragedy (for example, the fall of the tower of Siloam) and the sins of the people. Still, there is a connection between all of the violence and sin that all manifestations of the "culture of death" have in common. This is the insight we must rescue if we are to understand the religious origins, the religious roots of this tragedy and of the "culture of death" that surrounds us.

The journalist Andrew Sullivan also recognized the religious nature of what was happening in an article in *The New York Times Magazine*. Sullivan seems to claim that there is something inherent in the religious quest that is profoundly dangerous, namely, the quest for ultimate—and therefore absolute—truth, the search for an "all-explaining" reality. The danger in the quest for the absolute comes from thinking that one has found it, that one has grasped the mystery. Judaism, Christianity, and Islam are particularly prone to this danger because each one of them believes that the mystery has become somehow tied to a reality in this world: to a people and the Law in Judaism, to a Church and/or the Bible for Christians, and to the Islamic state and the Koran in Islam. Of these three, Sullivan considers Islam most prone to the danger because it has not gone through the evolution of modernity—namely, the secularist appeal to reasonable consensus as the test of the legitimate exercise of power. In any case, he argues, Islamic fundamentalism is no different from that of Christians and Jews. The real war that we are facing is not between religion and unbelief, but between religious fundamentalism and a faith that has embraced the tolerance required by reason. The United States, precisely as the most religious country in the world, is thus the very embodiment of religious tolerance that fundamentalists see as the enemy of God's authority over humankind.

Sullivan and others have equated the Islamic fundamentalism behind the acts of September 11 with the position of those who oppose abortion with violence. It is therefore important that we identify the origins of the dark side of religious convictions and hold fast to our own conviction that all manifestations of the "culture of death" have that same origin in the "sin of the world."

During the days following the horror of September 11, I re-read parts of Saint Augustine's *The City of God*, convinced that our situation vis-à-vis the modern world has many similarities to what Augustine lived and that *The City of God* is therefore an excellent source of insights into what our faith allows us to understand, the ultimate roots of what happens in the world in which we live.

Christians at the time of Saint Augustine were horrified at the barbarian destruction of Roman civilization, the sacking of the city of Rome. They were being accused by non-Christian Romans of not being able to protect the city from destruction as pagan religion had. As Augustine noted in a homily for the feast of Saints Peter and Paul, at that time the pagans—and the Christians secretly in their own hearts—were asking,

> Where are the tombs of the Apostles? Rome is desolate. Rome has become the victim of sacking. Rome has been conquered. Rome is occupied, handed over to the flames, with countless tragedies brought about by hunger, illness, and the sword. Where are the tombs of the Apostles?

That is, why weren't they able to protect us? Saint Augustine wrote *The City of God* to reply to this question, to reply to this accusation—so like what we hear now—that religions like Christianity that claim to possess the revelation of God are powerless to stop barbarians from destroying the best efforts of human civilization—if, in fact, they have not actually contributed to this destruction by fomenting religious wars and hatreds. That is why Saint Augustine's answers to these accusations are so important for us today, at the beginning of the third millennium of Christian history.

At the beginning of his Apostolic Letter *Novo Millennio Ineunte*, Pope John Paul II says that for us to understand adequately the challenge that our faith poses to our response to what is happening in this world at the dawn of the new millennium, we must remember above all that Christianity is grace. That is, the Christian vision of reality, of the ultimate roots of everything that surrounds us, does not originate in our prejudices, or pre-conceptions, or in ideas, philosophical convictions, and religious sensitivities. Our understanding of the ultimate roots of what happens in human life, both at the individual level and at the level of our societies, nations, and cultures, originates not in something we have discovered or concluded by the efforts of our intelligence and analysis but in something that has happened to us. It originates in an event—more precisely, in an encounter. This encounter is totally unforeseen and unplanned, and it bears absolutely no relation to anything in us that might prepare us for it. When it happens, it happens, period. It is not something that had to happen, and no one needs to be closer to or farther away from God for it to be able to happen. It happens as readily to good people as to people who act very badly, to religious people and to atheists, to people of any age, culture, or any other human configuration. This is what it means to say that this event is totally and purely gratuitous, that it is grace. Our response to this event, therefore, is always surprise, amazement, or wonder that gives rise to grace.

These are John Paul II's words:

> My thoughts turn first to the duty of *praise*. This is the point of departure for every genuine response of faith to the revelation of God in Christ. Christianity is grace. It is the wonder of a God who is not satisfied with creating the world and man, but puts himself on the same level as the creature he has made.

The unforeseen and unexpected appearance of God in human flesh, as our companion in human history, is the event that draws out of us that amazement, wonder, and praise that is the origin of our vision of the ultimate roots of what happens in our world, in precisely that same human history. The Christian view of the world, of human life, human history, and human events originates in our contemplation of the glory of God shining in the face—in the humanity—of Jesus Christ.

Again, John Paul II: "Contemplating Christ, we have also adored the Father and the Spirit, the one and undivided Trinity, the ineffable mystery in which everything has its origin and its fulfillment."

The conviction that everything in Christianity is grace is the basis for Saint Augustine's view of how to understand the roots of what is happening in the world around us. In the most famous passage in *The City of God*, he says that human existence is the life and history of two cities built by human beings, two cultures, two ways of life. He says that these two ways of life represent two different "loves" of which man is capable. "Two loves," he writes, "constructed two cities. The earthly city has been constructed by a love of self that leads to the contempt for God; the heavenly city has been constructed by a love for God that leads to the disdain for one's self."

Now, if we stopped here, as so many do, we would have completely misunderstood Saint Augustine; indeed, we would have completely contradicted his insight. He goes on to say, "Therefore, the earthly city sees its glory in itself; the other, the City of God, puts its glory [or has its consistency] in the Lord." *11*

The problem here lies in the expression *amor Dei usque ad contemptum sui*; the love that builds the City of God is said to be the "love of God as far as the contempt for self." It is important that we understand that this love is not a disdain for humankind, a hatred for sinful human beings. God cannot possibly require that. Such a God would not be the Father of mercies that we encounter in Jesus Christ, who leads us to love others, to love and respect human life, to live it to its fullest possibilities. Such a God would not be the God that loved the world so much that he sent his Son into it to share our life so that we could share his. Indeed, that God would be precisely the one who hates sinners and infidels and who orders them to be killed in order to affirm his rule or the God that does nothing about the deaths of thousands in order to show how sinful we have been.

The "disdain for self" of which Saint Augustine speaks is the result of that amazement or wonder at the inexpressible beauty and attraction of the revelation of God's glory in the humanity of Christ. It is the experience of a person who falls in love with someone and then forgets all about himself, forgets to have lunch or dinner in order to be with the one who has so attracted him. It's what happens when "you can't even watch *Star Trek*," as a scientist-companion of mine said to me back in the Sixties when he couldn't participate in our discussions about the show, which was in its first season, because he had fallen in love.

This attraction of grace, the attraction of this exceptional presence, makes one forget about oneself. The Christian disdain for self is the consequence of the overwhelming attraction of the mystery revealed in the humanity of Christ, that most precious of pearls that moves us to rid ourselves of all the other pearls in order to buy the field where it was found. It becomes manifest when we seek that glory and beauty and happiness for which our hearts were created, seek with every effort of which we are capable, every tactic we can think of, but without success. And then suddenly it is simply there—not as the fruit of our efforts but as an entirely free gift from a love we never suspected. That attraction is what moves us to build the City of God in this world.

Saint Augustine explains: "Human nature wounded by original sin generates the citizens of the earthly city." Let us pay attention: "human nature wounded by sin" is the origin of our tragedy, our violence, our destructiveness, our anti-life culture. *Naturam peccato uitiatam*, human nature mysteriously wounded; our mind, our intelligence, our vision of reality, our will, our freedom mysteriously wounded by a reality that for lack of a better word we call "original sin," something that is not inherent to human nature as God created it, something that does not define what it means to be really human but in fact contradicts it—this is the origin of what Augustine calls the "earthly city." This is the root of our problem, the root of the culture of violence and death.

We can never forget it. When we—though horrified by all the violence in the world, by all the attacks against innocent life—nevertheless avoid the temptation to explain them away with incomplete, insufficient, erroneous explanations, and when we acknowledge that in Christ we have experienced what God is like and what we were created for—that we have contemplated the beauty and have been grasped by the attraction of grace—then we will recognize that without that grace we too have, deep within ourselves, that same wound in our human nature, and we too are capable of such violence. This is the Christian reaction to September 11 and the Christian reaction to all the manifestations of hatred and violence found in the world.

Hence, Saint Augustine:

> The grace that frees human nature from sin gives birth to the heavenly city, so that while those [the citizens of the other city] are called vessels full of anger [*vasa irae*, "vessels full of ire"], these [the citizens of the heavenly city] are called vessels full of mercy [*vasa misericordiae*].

This is a magnificent observation. Anger or mercy, these are the two alternatives, the two human energies that build the two cultures. The "culture of death" is built by anger, while the culture of life is built by mercy. Therefore, mercy, and not anger, should be our motivation in our efforts against the violence against life so widespread in our world today.

Our world, exactly as in the time of Augustine, can be a world guided by a declared or undeclared atheism, or it can be guided by cynicism, the refusal to deal with the ultimate questions about the origin and final destiny of human life, or it can be guided by an effort to restrict those questions to the private realm, allowing them no part in the formulation of public policy, or it can be inspired by a religion so sentimentalized that it becomes pathological.

Whatever the case, from the perspective of the Christian faith, each of these alternatives is completely insufficient to satisfy the deepest desires and hopes of the human heart that was created to be moved and guided by the grace, the attraction of God's glory in Christ, a grace that can appear as if out of nowhere, whatever the condition or ethical stature of the world in which we live, because it is a saving grace that takes away the sin of the world. And it is only in being moved by this grace, by this attraction, this wonder, this amazement, that we will build the City of God, the heavenly city in the midst of this very world—not with the power of anger, the violence of anger, but with the power, the attraction, of the mercy that has invaded our hearts, hearts otherwise tempted by, and capable of, the same violence as anybody else's heart.

Augustine was writing this during the regime of a great Christian emperor, Theodosius, whom he admired greatly. Do you know why he admired him? Because for Saint Augustine, the first duty of a Catholic politician, a Catholic leader in society, is that he recognize himself to be a sinner. The non-Christian emperor or leader could or could not be a very religious person, he could believe in the highest human virtues, but that doesn't matter. The difference between such a leader and a Christian one is that the Christian one knows that he is a sinner. What Augustine admired in Theodosius was not that he promoted laws and practices that corresponded to Christian moral principles; what made Theodosius a Christian leader in Augustine's eyes was the humility with which Theodosius accepted the public penance that all sinners accept as a sign of their prayer for God's mercy. The key point, he said, is not that those who exercise political power should be persons following the highest moral principles; the key point is that they not force us to do evil, that they allow us to follow the attraction of grace.

Indeed, as Augustine says,

> These two cities are mixed together in the world. . . . The redeemed family of Christ the Lord and the pilgrim city on earth belonging to Christ the King defends itself from those who would destroy it, but let it know that among those who consider themselves its enemies, there are those, who cannot be identified, who one day will be among its own citizens.

In such a perspective, it is impossible in theory to contemplate any kind of crusade in order to rid the world of the enemies of God's City. Instead, Augustine writes:

> It should not appear as fruitless to put up with these enemies until some of them recognize the same grace that we have recognized. . . . This is true because, also within the City of God, as long as it is still a pilgrim in this world, there are citizens which, though (visibly) united now in the reception of the same sacraments (*conexos communione sacramentorum*), will not be its citizens forever.

These latter are those who are not moved by the grace of the Holy Spirit.

Again, "Christianity is grace," as John Paul II reminded us, echoing the wonderful words of Saint Thérèse of Lisieux: "Everything is grace." This is what allows us to recognize the roots of what's happening and to respond accordingly, not by trying to be the saviors of this world through our efforts, our good deeds, our politics, our teachings, but by being the vehicles through which the grace of Christ can shine and exercise its attraction to those in the earthly city called to it, which is everyone, since God wants all to be saved, as Saint Paul wrote.

We do this by remaining faithful to the event of the appearance of God's grace in Christ and being guided by its overwhelming attraction, following it in our individual and public lives—our lives as citizens, our political life, our professional life, our life as parents, spouses, or sons and daughters, as students and workers, as healthy or sick, young or old, rich or poor—all the time aware that without this grace, we ourselves would be no different from the ones bringing about all the violence.

All human beings are moved by whatever they think gives meaning and value to life. The search for that ultimate measure of the value and meaning of life is called religion. All human beings are moved by this religious sense, however it is that they conceive of this ultimate reality, this mystery, whether they acknowledge it as a mystery and call it God, or whether they call it something else—like values or ideals—and imagine that it originates in human nature.

But in the end, it is inevitable that this religious sense will become more and more frustrated, because it never gets to the expected happiness, it never reaches what it seeks. In its frustration, the religious sense will build its own idols and become angry at whatever threatens or seems to be different, whatever threatens the false security for which the decaying religious sense is forced to settle in its frustration. Thus it leads to anger and intolerance. The rejection of religion is itself a religious position worshipping another idol, and therefore also eventually leads to anger and intolerance and violence against those who will not share its idolatry.

Listen to how realistic Saint Augustine is about this. There are two idols, he says, two types of idols that, in its frustration, the earthly city sets up for its worship. One is whatever gives pleasure to the body. The pleasures of the body are wonderful, good experiences. The problem is that, not having found what it seeks, the earthly city idealizes these pleasures, that is, converts them into idols, into the ultimate purpose of life, and sacrifices everything else to them. Surely, we can recognize this as a powerful obstacle to the defense of the sacredness of human life today.

But listen to the second type of idol that, according to Augustine, is as much an obstacle (if not more so) to the recognition of the ultimate truth and purpose of human life. Saint Augustine says that idols emerge also from the idealization of the moral virtues! The very moral ideas by which we try to live are idealized and set up as idols. It reminds me of Flannery O'Connor's claim that today the value of tenderness has become so idealized, so "detached from its root" (which she identified as Christ), that it has become an empty sentiment, an empty emotion that is actually dangerous, indeed deadly, because in its name we kill those whom we pity because we cannot make their lives be as we think they should be.

This is also what Walker Percy suggests when he says that one could be a "theoretician of mankind" (that is, someone who thinks he has discovered what human life is all about) and maybe stumble onto some useful insights, or a "lover of mankind" (as an idea, a concept) and maybe actually do some good for concrete human beings. But, he says, if you are both a theoretician of mankind and a lover of mankind, you are deadly dangerous, because in the name of love, or compassion, or tenderness you will eliminate those whose lives do not fit the definition of what you claim human life should be like.

This is the root of our problem. This is what it is all about: a derailed religious sense that has not encountered the miracle of grace. As the eccentric priest says at the end of Percy's *The Thanatos Syndrome* in his homily to the health-care practitioners promoting abortion and euthanasia and genetic engineering, the terrible problem, the satanic horror of it all, is not that they are bad people, but that they are good people, very good people, committed to humanity's well-being. This is what Augustine means when he says that the wonderful moral values of the earthly city are greater obstacles to the recognition of grace than the idealized pleasures of the body.

And it is also possible to claim to be a Christian but follow an idealized picture of Christ—not the real, historical Jesus of Nazareth present in the flesh in the life of the Church. It is possible to follow Christ as a great teacher, a great example, an inspiration, and to live by so-called "Christian values." That too is an obstacle to grace, an idol. Writing to an adherent of Pelagianism, the doctrine of salvation by our own moral efforts, Augustine says: "This is the horrible and hidden poison of your error, that you hold the grace of Christ to consist in his example, and not in the gift of his person." And again, John Paul II: "We shall not be saved by a formula, but by a person."

Even the earthly city, says Augustine, has its faith, a human faith. It has the human hope of avoiding evils. Even the earthly city wishes and hopes for what is good and has a fragile love for true goodness. Saint Augustine looks upon all of its efforts, including its mistakes, not with anger, but with great pity and compassion. But our faith is different, he says: *diversa fide, diversa spe, diverso amore.* What makes it different is simply that our faith, hope, and love are born of the attraction of grace, are born of the experience of wonder and praise.

I conclude with the words of John Paul II:

> "What must we do?" We put the question with trusting optimism, but without underestimating the problems we face. We are certainly not seduced by the naive expectation that, faced with the great challenges of our time, we shall find some magic formula. No, we shall not be saved by a formula, but by a Person, and the assistance which he gives us: I am with you! It is not therefore a matter of inventing a "new program." The program already exists. It is the plan found in the Gospel and in the living Tradition. It is the same as ever. Ultimately it has its center in Christ himself, who is to be known, loved and imitated, so that in him we may live the life of the Trinity, and with him transform history until its fulfillment in the heavenly Jerusalem.

Between Now and Eternity

Faith, Politics, and the Encounter with Christ

IN DEALING WITH THE PROBLEM of faith and politics, we must first define what exactly faith is. We have endless discussions about faith and politics, but they are useless because we are using the word faith in different ways. Politics is easier to understand because we know it from experience; we know that it is simply exercising the right to determine how government will direct the distribution of power in a society to bring about the common good. It's not a mysterious thing. The problem is faith.

To understand the view of faith and politics proposed by the Catholic Church, it is important to distinguish between faith and the religious sense. The discussion of religion and politics is not the same as the discussion about faith and politics.

The religious sense is our conviction, our experience, of whatever it is that ties this moment in our lives with existence, with our final destiny. It's the mystery of how and why we are here. It's what to do with the world that surrounds us. It's how to obtain satisfaction of the needs that we all experience in relation to the world that is out there seemingly to satisfy those needs.

Politics, in that sense, is a manifestation of the religious sense. It's an attempt to make sense of life and to satisfy our needs. You cannot separate politics from the religious sense. And in that way, there'll be many religious senses around. The religions of the world are all different ways of carrying out this search, of expressing this need, and politics is the art of making sure that all of them make a contribution and don't wipe each other out.

What would you expect from a politics that is a response to the religious perspective? You would expect a politics that will not provoke, or bring about, the silencing of the religious search. In that sense, all that religious people need from the world of politics is religious liberty: the openness to the search and then the ability to make a contribution to society based on this opening to infinity. And so the most important requirement to be made of politics or any government is religious freedom. Without this, we cannot proceed.

That already presents a problem in many areas of the world, perhaps even in our own society, one that is dedicated to religious freedom. At an elementary level, we look to see how that is being lived in our society today. And we obviously favor those political proposals that respect and promote this religious freedom. Those that do not already demonstrate a form of inhumanity.

There are various ways of violating the religious quest, of violating religious freedom. If we understand religion as the relation between time and the eternal, between now and destiny, then one way to violate this religious freedom is to choose either side to the exclusion of the other.

Choosing the "now" is secularism—an ideology that doesn't allow the human openness to infinity to play an important part in life, both individual and social, and therefore in political life. Secularism is an ideology that is present to the degree to which it excludes religious concerns from the public square, in its program of discussion and education, etc. That's one way of violating religious freedom.

Another way of violating religious freedom is by choosing "eternity" and having it prevail in its interests, such as they may be (though one wonders how one ever arrives at the interests of eternity). Eternity, in this case, rules what happens at the present time—it's a form of theocracy. Perhaps it's not our biggest danger, but it is present in this age.

We have seen, and we're always aware, that we can have either one of these two scenarios. We must reject both. We must reject a separation of "now" and "eternity" in order to make one dominate the other. But if that's the case, then how do I relate the two? How do I relate those interests within me that deal with my search for happiness—for justice, truth, for the fulfillment of the desires of my heart, my openness to infinity—how do I relate all of that to the concrete needs of the moment, what I need to do now, how I judge what's going on today? I know that I can't exclude either pole, but how do I ever bring them together?

What happens next is an attempt at compromise. The relation between the two will be simply the best that can be expected. It will be redefined every election time, every time that the question arises. But the problem with compromise is that it's finally impossible. The religious sense always wants to move towards infinity, and the desire to do that makes it dangerous to the political world, which also wants to move in the same direction. It wants to embrace everything. So then the question becomes: How do we design a situation that is not in conflict?

My answer to that is that, with one exception, it's not possible. The two sides are in conflict. And in the end, a compromise is the best that we can do. I am prepared to say that between the religious sense and earthly politics there is a conflict and that the experience of that conflict will not go away—except for one case. The efforts to solve the problem of religion and politics—not to mention that the problem is worsened when you move from religion to faith, which I will get to in a moment—are useless. We can't solve them.

The only solution to the problem of time and eternity, limited and unlimited, finite and infinite—the only "solution" to that problem is Jesus Christ. That is the statement that we must be prepared to make. Only the knowledge of, the experience of, the encounter with Christ, can resolve the problem between time and eternity and therefore between religion and politics.

Are we prepared to make that statement? This is the first problem. This is where all our claims begin to fall to the ground. We hesitate to say that only Christ is the solution to this conflict. What are we afraid of? Why would I hesitate to say that this is the only solution to the human problem?

Because we are both in time and made for eternity, the only solution is Christ. From the very beginning, we are created to discover in Christ the fulfillment of all the aspects of our creation. I adhere to the teaching in the Bible and the teaching of the Church—especially in the Second Vatican Council, in *Gaudium et Spes* 22, which John Paul II made his motto, and his teaching in *Redemptor Hominis*—on the centrality of Christ, that only in Christ is the mystery of what it is to be human revealed. Only in Christ is the relation between religion and politics understood.

Are we prepared to say that and to explore its implications?

Jesus Christ is one reality, and a very particular one. He is the one reality—the particular, the single instance that gives meaning to the totality: the Incarnation. Some people are not willing to say that. That's why they are not Christians. And I can understand that. What's difficult to understand is calling oneself a Christian and being afraid to say it.

We do not have the problem, or the mission, to construct a bridge between faith and politics. To attempt to solve this problem already violates our humanity. Every single attempt to build this bridge has been a weakening of faith, or a betrayal of the Incarnation. And historically, there have been many attempts.

Now, faith intensifies the problem because faith—unlike the religious sense, which is the search for the infinite mystery without which we cannot live—identifies this mystery with the reality of this world, with a very concrete, particular reality.

With the religious sense there is no direct conflict with the political order unless there is a demand that one particular religious experience rules. But faith makes a statement like the one I just made, that only Christ brings about the solution of the human problem. And by Christ I don't mean another synonym for "God," but I mean a particular human being who lived in a particular place in a particular time. I am not using Christ's name here as did the Greeks in the Acts of the Apostles, as a name for the infinite, the unknown, the invisible God. I am talking about a particular man in a particular moment in history. To recognize that this man is the embodiment and the presence of the mystery—that is faith.

For us as Christians, faith is the recognition that this one man, Jesus Christ, is the revelation, the disclosure, the unveiling, of the destiny and origin of all that exists. That is to say, this is what it means to proclaim that Jesus Christ is God—that this man is that. Once we make that claim, we have no idea of—we can't even begin to imagine—a God without Christ. For us, it no longer makes sense.

The discourse in which we try to separate our convictions about Christ from God is already flawed because we do not know any other God but the one that is revealed in Christ. That is what the faith is. It is a conviction that there is no God but the one that is revealed in Jesus Christ. Again, when we make that statement, as the Vatican declaration *Dominus Iesu* did, it creates a riot. (I can understand it creating a riot outside Christianity. But within Christianity? Within the Catholic Church itself?)

There are other faiths. There are other proposals that tie the mystery to an earthly reality. Judaism, from which our faith derives, ties it to the election and formation of a people. Such people will relate to the destiny, to eternity, by means of the experience of belonging to a chosen people. This will affect their relation to politics, as you can see throughout the Old Testament. There was no separation between politics and the identity of the people as chosen by God. The whole dispute was about that—back and forth about fidelity to the covenant, infidelity to the covenant. World history was experienced and understood in terms of that drama, again and again.

When, for example, Israel, under some of its leaders, would want to form an alliance with a particular nation to defend itself, a prophet would arrive (who was never very popular) and say "No, this is not going to save you." He would say "You must trust in the covenant. You make that alliance, and you're going to be through." Or the Lord would raise up their enemies to bring home the point and allow all kinds of things to happen. Again and again, fidelity to the covenant has formed that people. It is the key to the relation between faith and politics in Israel even today.

The second such phenomenon is Islam. As we know, in the Islamic world today, there is a great discussion about faith and politics that ranges from an awareness that this relation has to be worked out to an extremism of the kind we face. But there's no question that the problem is not religion and politics, but faith, that in this religion God passes through the God that is revealed in the Koran, who in fact has dictated it. And in the Koran are found many political proposals about how to organize society and the world and how to judge these realities.

The third proposal of how to tie the mystery to an earthly reality is Christianity. For us, the mystery, the destiny, the eternal, is embodied in one man, Jesus of Nazareth. In some ways, the relation between faith and politics is a manifestation of Christology. Traditionally we try to understand how humanity and divinity are related in this one man. That is what Christology is. And this Christological debate has immense political consequences because this one man, we claim, is the link between our present life and our final destiny.

When we, for example, talk about the fundamental contribution that the Church has made to the culture concerning personal freedom, the very existence of personhood as a unique and irreplaceable individual—a "who" which is not exhausted by a "what"—that insight is the result of the Christological debate that led to the Council of Chalcedon in the fifth century. It was there that the Church was finally able to find a way of expressing this conviction about who Christ is. Until then it could not be understood because the concept of personhood that existed was insufficient. The Church had to invent the concept of personhood, perhaps its greatest contribution. But it did not invent it in the process of developing a political philosophy. It invented it by trying to understand who Christ is. For us the relation between faith and politics is a branch of Christology. If we have problems with Christology, we have to deal with those before we have anything to say. We are not speaking as Christians, as Catholics, to this world if it doesn't come from that conviction.

Christianity began when a bunch of people encountered this man Jesus Christ. No one sat down to design a Christology. It doesn't emerge from any particular system of thought. It was a fact, an encounter. That's how it begins. You meet this man and something happens. If we cannot grasp that, then what follows is just concepts. Our claims that the relation between faith and politics is a branch of Christology and that Christology starts with an encounter with Christ mean that we will not grasp nor make a Catholic proposal about the relation between faith and politics unless we share its point of origin, which is the experience of the encounter with Christ. This started it all, and this is what sustains it all. A proposal that doesn't come from that experience has no power. It's just words if it doesn't start with that fact.

Now, there is a further problem. How do I today experience this encounter with Christ that is going to lead me to a new, unexpected, unimaginable vision of life, of what is possible, the vision of destiny for which we are created? How is that possible today? The Christian world divides in answering that question. That is why you have Catholic politics, Protestant politics, and fundamentalist politics. They're different because of the different ways each version lives the encounter with Christ. In his book *Why the Church?*, Giussani mentions three possible ways of having an encounter with Christ.

The first is the way of rationalism, which is the study and scientific reflection on historical documents and tradition. Many people, many Christians today, follow that way. Of course, it leads to academic debates that are never resolved and to uncertainty because the figure of Jesus disappears or becomes almost overwhelmingly irrelevant, and you appear stupid for wanting to hang on to it or trying to explain what Jesus would say about nuclear weapons. The rationalist way is not an event and it has no power.

The second is individual inspiration, associated more or less with the Protestant way. A direct link with Christ will determine your politics. Unfortunately, it will make it very difficult for you to speak to people who don't have that link to Christ, who haven't experienced it.

The third, the Catholic way, is the claim that the experience of the encounter with Christ is today the experience of belonging to a people whose life is the expression of Christ's victory. The experience of the fact of who he is has implications in terms of our life. And we can judge political proposals, economic proposals, just as we are supposed to judge our own individual lives in the areas of work, vocation, faith, based on the guidance that this experience gives us.

Our political proposals will return to the event of Christ, the fact, to the way it is encountered today, to the community called the Church, to the presence in this world of this way of living together and judging reality together, and how this is sustained—the Magisterium, the sacraments—what defines the Church as a visible reality, a society. We even use the word society, a people. Peoplehood is at the origin, for it is a peoplehood expressed as a society and structured as an institution. It is a recognizable reality, just as Jesus was recognizable as a particular human being. If the particularity of the Church offends us, given its universal claims, then why aren't we offended by the particularity of Jesus? He was just one man. The Church at least can put on an impressive show. Jesus was one man who was killed.

We want to look at the moment we are living through and its political dimensions in terms of what has happened to us in the encounter with Christ and our lived reality of the mystery of the Church. We cannot be separated from the Church because the presence of Christ today, of his victory, is this form of coming together.

In this way, two fundamental values immediately become absolutely clear. We will favor that which promotes the liberty of the

Church to carry on its work. Freedom is the experience of the fact that I am, in that moment, and in that location, walking towards the satisfaction—the real satisfaction—of all the desires of my life. It is what makes me free. This is the freedom we propose.

And we oppose, no matter what—no matter what—anything that threatens the unity of the Church. Anything from any politician, any party, in domestic politics, or foreign policy, or whatever it is, anything that tries to create division within the Church, we must oppose, because unity and its compatibility with our freedom, this is the victory of Christ! Because if that disappears, then Christ is not victorious and we have no solution to the problem of faith and politics and the only solution to religion and politics is just an unsatisfactory compromise.

Only Wonder Knows

On Being a Scientist and a Believer

I BEGAN PREPARING TO WRITE this during the Christmas season. Sometimes I reflected on the relation between science and faith, and other times I thought about the meaning of Christmas. According to my Latin American, Spanish, and Puerto Rican cultural tradition—at least when I was growing up—the heart of Christmas was the Solemnity of the Epiphany, or as we called it: *La Venida de los Tres Santos Reyes Magos* (the coming of the three holy "magician" kings). In Spain, this is the day children receive their presents from the kings, though in Puerto Rico we also expected gifts from Santa Claus on Christmas Day, and many times he proved to be more generous than the three holy kings, who also required food for their camels in exchange for their gifts.

At one point in my musings, however, the two topics came together in my thought and it occurred to me that it would be interesting if I offered to you my thoughts on science and faith in terms of the Biblical account of the encounter between the Magi and the newborn Jesus.

> In the time of King Herod, after Jesus was born in Bethlehem of Judea, wise men from the East came to Jerusalem, asking, "Where is the child who has been born king of the Jews? For we observed his star at its rising and have come to pay him homage." When King Herod heard this, he was frightened, and all Jerusalem with him; and calling together all the chief priests and scribes of the people, he inquired of them where the Messiah was to be born. They told him, "In Bethlehem of Judea; for so it has been written by the prophet: 'And you, Bethlehem, in the land of Judah, are by no means least among the rulers of Judah; for from you shall come a ruler who is to

shepherd my people Israel.'" Then Herod secretly called for the wise men and learned from them the exact time when the star had appeared. Then he sent them to Bethlehem, saying, "Go and search diligently for the child; and when you have found him, bring me word so that I may also go and pay him homage." When they had heard the king, they set out; and there, ahead of them, went the star that they had seen at its rising, until it stopped over the place where the child was. When they saw that the star had stopped, they were overwhelmed with joy. On entering the house, they saw the child with Mary his mother; and they knelt down and paid him homage. Then, opening their treasure chests, they offered him gifts of gold, frankincense, and myrrh. And having been warned in a dream not to return to Herod, they left for their own country by another path (Mt 2:1–12).

Who were these mysterious figures, the Magi, popularly referred to as wise men and kings?

The word Magi is a Latinization of the plural of the Greek word *magos*, itself from Old Persian *maguŝ*, referring to the priestly caste of Zoroastrianism. As part of their religion, these priests paid particular attention to the stars and gained an international reputation for astrology, which was at that time highly regarded as a science. Their religious practices and use of astrology caused derivatives of the term *magi* to be applied to the occult in general and led to the English term *magic*. Translated in the King James Version as *wise men*, the same translation is applied to the wise men led by Daniel in the Hebrew Scriptures. The same word is also translated as *sorcerer* when describing "Elymas the sorcerer" and Simon Magus, considered a heretic by the early Church, both mentioned in the Acts of the Apostles.

The Zoroastrian Magi in Matthew's Gospel were indeed motivated by religious reasons to study the stars, but their studies themselves were pursued without religious prejudices. They were searching for laws of nature that reveal an order, a *logos*, a cosmos with a permanent structure that dispels the fear of chaos present in primordial experiences of the mystery of existence. In that sense, they were scientists.

In his commentary on Matthew's gospel, Erasmo Leiva-Merikakis writes:

> Like good scientists, the Magi take a more cosmic, a more all-encompassing view of things. In these pagans we encounter

a perfect unity between patient science and moral justice. . . .
the wise man seeks truth, and when he finds it, he does not
hesitate to adore it, to subject himself to it.

This suggests that adoration is the end of all scientific and philo-
sophic pursuits.

Another characteristic of the Magi's discovery of the new star is
joy—not merely a mental satisfaction, as when solving a problem or
finding an answer to a problem, but an existential satisfaction, an interior vibration of the heart filled with wonder at the existence of a
reality that is revealing its secrets, so to speak. What true scientist has
not experienced this joy, this wonder, this awe before a deeper knowledge of reality?

The question we face today is whether this experience of a joyful wonder is possible or whether we have to resign ourselves to a
relativism that reduces everything—scientific research included—
to subjectivism.

Consider the observations of Jonah Lehrer in an article in *The New
Yorker* magazine "The Truth Wears Off: Is there Something Wrong
with the Scientific Method?":

> On September 18, 2007, a few dozen neuroscientists, psy-
> chiatrists, and drug-company executives gathered in a hotel
> conference room in Brussels to hear some startling news. It
> had to do with a class of drugs known as atypical or second-
> generation antipsychotics, which came on the market in the
> early nineties. The drugs. . . had been tested on schizophrenics
> in several large clinical trials, all of which had demonstrated a
> dramatic decrease in the subjects' psychiatric symptoms. As
> a result, second-generation antipsychotics had become one
> of the fastest-growing and most profitable pharmaceutical
> classes.

The data presented at the Brussels meeting made it clear that
something strange was happening: the therapeutic power of the drugs
appeared to be steadily waning. A recent study showed an effect that
was less than half of that documented in the first trials in the early
1990s. Many researchers began to argue that the expensive pharmaceu-
ticals weren't any better than first-generation antipsychotics, which
have been in use since the Fifties.

Before the effectiveness of a drug can be confirmed, it must be tested and tested again. Different scientists in different labs need to repeat the protocols and publish their results. The test of replicability, as it's known, is the foundation of modern research. Replicability is how the community enforces itself. It's a safeguard for the creep of subjectivity. Most of the time, scientists know what results they want, and that can influence the results they get. The premise of replicability is that the scientific community can correct for these flaws.

But now all sorts of well-established, multiply-confirmed findings have started to look increasingly uncertain. It's as if our facts were losing their truth: claims that have been enshrined in textbooks are suddenly unprovable. This phenomenon doesn't yet have an official name, but it's occurring across a wide range of fields.

For many scientists, the effect is especially troubling because of what it exposes about the scientific process. If replication is what separates the rigor of science from the squishiness of pseudoscience, where do we put all these rigorously validated findings that can no longer be proven? Which results should we believe? Francis Bacon, the early-modern philosopher and pioneer of the scientific method, once declared that experiments were essential, because they allowed us to "put nature to the question." But it appears that nature often gives us different answers.

This suggests that the decline effect is actually a decline of illusion. Many scientific theories continue to be considered true even after failing numerous experimental tests. Even the law of gravity hasn't always been perfect at predicting real-world phenomena. (In one test, physicists measuring gravity by means of deep boreholes in the Nevada desert found a two-and-a-half-percent discrepancy between the theoretical predictions and the actual data.)

Such anomalies demonstrate the slipperiness of empiricism. Although many scientific ideas generate conflicting results and suffer from falling effect sizes, they continue to get cited in the textbooks and drive standard medical practice. Why? Because these ideas seem true. Because they make sense. Because we can't bear to let them go. And this is why the decline effect is so troubling. Not because it reveals the human fallibility of science, in which data are tweaked and beliefs shape perceptions. (Such shortcomings aren't surprising, at least for scientists.) And not because it reveals that many of our most exciting theories are fleeting fads and will soon be rejected. (That idea has been around since Thomas Kuhn.)

The decline effect is troubling because it reminds us how difficult it is to prove anything. We like to pretend that our experiments define the truth for us. But that's often not the case. Just because an idea is true doesn't mean it can be proven. And just because an idea can be proven doesn't mean it's true. When the experiments are done, we still have to choose what to believe.

In such a case, are awe, wonder, and joy at scientific discoveries possible?

When I was thinking about this, a friend sent me the text of a speech given by Giussani about the "love of being" that is remarkably appropriate to this reflection.

Giussani's argument is that the truth of Christianity can be verified by a proper consideration of the evidence for it. Evidence, he says, is the correct word, even if the evidence for the Christian claim is given to us through signs. Signs are things that can be touched, seen, and experienced. The Apostles had Jesus in front of them, and this presence was a sign of his victory over death and therefore of his mysterious identity. But what about us? What happens with the passage of time? What signs are there for us as evidence of the truth of the Christian claim, of the reasonableness of the Christian claim?

The interpretation of the signs available to us engages our liberty, he says. In this drama, our liberty is a manifestation of our love for being. Without this love for being we are not truly free, and we will never grasp the evidence of the signs given to us. At this point, as an example of this love for being, Giussani invokes the Magi.

He asks why the Magi decided to pursue the sign of the star. Why did they follow the impulse that they felt within themselves when they saw the star? "Because they were full of love for Being," he answers. This is the characteristic of those who are poor in spirit, he continues. One who is poor in spirit is like a child who says yes to everything that is evidently present before him. It is a matter of not imposing our expectations to block our recognition that something unforeseen is happening, that it has happened, and it is worthwhile to pursue its meaning.

This is what made the Magi take off on their journey, this opening or poverty of spirit, this child-like fascination, amazement, awe. The sign of the star, so to speak, unveiled a path to follow, a road to take.

What determined this road for them, as they traveled day and night on their camels with their presents, as they rested at night looking at the sky because they were perhaps not sleepy? What determined their way? It was following the path of the star they could see.

Still, recall that at one moment the star disappeared. Why did they continue their search? Why not give up and go back home, losing interest in the search, figuring they had made a mistake? The star was gone, their enthusiasm low or gone, and yet they continued. Obviously, it had not been the star itself, or their intelligent calculations, or their imagination, or their enthusiasm that moved them: it was something that had happened, that they could not rationally deny had happened. The reason for their search was a kind of "benevolence," says Giussani, a benevolence that guided them. The reason for following the road, the motivation, that which defined the road, was the initial event, that which had made them take off on their journey, and they could not go back on it, because *factum infectum fieri nequit*, you cannot make something that happened become something that has not happened.

And so it is this poverty of spirit, this interior simplicity, this lack of fear that innocence has, this spirit of the beggar that begs for the spiritual nourishment that truth communicates, this love for being that opens us up to the grace of the gift of faith that allows us to recognize the truth of the mystery of Being.

Is this not also at the root of scientific research, a love for science that protects it from the relativism that now threatens it?

But, to ask again, is such an interior disposition possible today?

I recall the words of my friend Robert Pollack, Professor of Biological Sciences and Director of the Center for the Study of Science and Religion at Columbia University, in his talk "Science Informed by Awe." Bob starts the day with the Jewish prayer: "The beginning of wisdom is awe of the Lord" (in the book of Job we also read: "The fear of the Lord that is wisdom, and to depart from evil is understanding"). This awe, he said, was understood as awe before the grandeur of nature, before its incomprehensibility, as in Psalm 92, recited by the Levitical priesthood in the Temple on Shabbat: "How vast are your works, Lord; your designs are beyond our grasp." However, according to Pollack, in this age of science, we no longer have the luxury of this "incomprehensibility."

Consider this:

I am not exaggerating the seriousness of this problem: scientific insight into the meaninglessness of DNA-based life is not simply missing meaning. It is a demonstration that a satisfactory, even elegant explanation of the workings of this aspect of nature actually conflicts with the assumption of purpose and meaning.

Pollack thinks that poets can understand this better than those not as skilled in self-awareness. He quotes from Edna St. Vincent Millay's poem "Spring":

> To what purpose April, do you return again?. . .
> The smell of the earth is good.
> It is apparent that there is no death.
> But what does that signify?
> Not only under ground are the brains of men
> Eaten by maggots.
> Life in itself
> Is nothing,
> An empty cup, a flight of uncarpeted stairs.
> It is not enough that yearly, down this hill,
> April
> Comes like an idiot, babbling and strewing flowers.

Still, Pollack sees grounds for awe in the human ethical choices, which are inexplicable in terms of nature, to freely perform actions on behalf of another that "slip the constraints of natural selection." During a visit to a house where professional women lived in community, freely embracing a life of poverty, virginity, and obedience, Pollack said to me that to freely choose such a life was an example of escaping the boundaries of natural selection.

"That is also the intersect of awe and science," he concluded, and thus, I suggest, the path to a faith that expands the scope of reason beyond what scientific rationality allows. Once again, the capacity to experience awe or wonder is the path to the knowledge of reality made possible by faith.

This, of course, was known already by Saint Gregory of Nyssa in the fourth century. In *The Life of Moses* he writes: "Concepts create idols; only wonder [or awe] knows." In an essay titled "Only Wonder Knows" Giussani insists again that the capacity for wonder requires simplicity of heart and poverty of spirit, the attitude of a child who, upon seeing something new (like a new star in the sky), reaches out to it to touch it, to explore it without any "ifs" or "buts." Wonder is the experience that John and Andrew had when they first saw Jesus and decided to follow him.

Faith is the affirmation of a fact, of the objectivity of a fact from which there emanates an aesthetic dimension, a suggestiveness that demonstrates human reason in action. Goodness or ethics, writes Giussani, derives from aesthetics. Otherwise, morality is alienating, because it doesn't correspond to the desire of the heart that makes us human; it doesn't generate amazement, wonder, or awe, but leads instead to fear or boredom. Sacrifices required by preconceptions are destructive of the self; only a sacrifice motivated by wonder, awe, by an unexpected attractiveness of a Presence is consistent with being fully human.

Thomas Aquinas put it bluntly: without grace, the law of Christ is deadly. What is grace if not gracefulness, gentility. . . yes, beauty to be discovered in nature in spite of the meaninglessness of the results of evolutionary science?

Can a scientist of today meet the requirements of modern science and still be a believer? The answer, I propose, is not only *yes he can*, but, in fact, it is faith that will sustain his or her passion for investigating nature and prevent the process itself and its results from becoming enslaved to political, economic, and religious ideology.

IV. THE RELEVANCE OF THE STARS

God at *The New Yorker*

Faith, Reason, and the Varieties of Secular Experience

IN 1999, THE CARDINAL Archbishop of New York, John O'Connor, invited me to be a visiting professor of theology at the archdiocesan seminary. He also asked me to help in two areas of Church life in the archdiocese: the Hispanic apostolate and the possible establishment of an archdiocesan office for faith and culture.

Cardinal O'Connor was familiar with my work for the international Catholic movement Communion and Liberation, for which the relation between faith and culture is of central concern. Father Luigi Giussani, an Italian priest, founded this movement in 1954 when his work with young people led him to the conclusion that, in spite of the apparent strength of the Catholic Church at that time in Italy, for these young people the Catholic faith was merely a source of abstract ideas and values that had no relation to their experience of life.

In response to this situation and convinced that faith devoid of experience will not produce culture, Father Giussani left his work as a seminary professor of theology to teach at a high school in order to reach young people at a time when they were forming their own view of what life is all about. He had no intentions of organizing a movement. Communion and Liberation was born simply from the impact his experience had on his students.

Today, the movement is found in all parts of the world, with communities made up of people of all ages, cultures, and areas of work. The way in which the experience of faith generates a culture remains one of its major areas of concern. In the early 1990s, Father Giussani had asked me to help the communities in the United States to understand better the American religious experience and its effect on what has become, in fact, the dominant culture of the world. Cardinal O'Connor was familiar with my involvement with this effort, hence his interest in seeing what could be done in New York.

Soon after I arrived in New York, a friend from Washington, DC., who writes for the liberal weekly *The New Republic*, held a dinner to welcome me to the city. Among the guests were several of his friends from the secular media, among them Hendrik Hertzberg, a writer and editor at *The New Yorker*. When he learned about my work studying the thought of Pope John Paul II, Rick invited me to a few lunches with him and other editors to discuss the possibility of writing an article about the then upcoming visit of Pope John Paul II to Cuba. The result was the cover article that I wrote for the January 26, 1998 issue, "The Poet and the Revolutionary."

In less than a year after my arrival in New York I had written a cover article for *The New Yorker*.

It was my first experience of the profound interest in secular media circles in the challenges to modern culture posed by the personal life experiences of John Paul II who—as a former poet, actor, dramatist, and modern philosopher—appeared to belong to their intellectual world.

Of course, as I expected, among these journalists and intellectuals there was almost total rejection of his teachings in such areas as sexual morality, the ordination of women, and liberation theology. Still, it was evident that the pope had struck a chord in their hearts with a challenge to their radical secularism in the name of a devotion to the humanism they sought to profess.

Rick invited me to join a group of friends that met every week to discuss contemporary issues, all of whom shared his secular, liberal perspective. My role in these meetings, I suppose, was to represent the interests of the "Invisible Mystery," or something like that. I found that although we differed greatly in our approach to many of the issues under discussion, we shared many of the same fundamental concerns.

In all of my interventions during the discussions, I tried to show the relationship between what my faith teaches me and those shared concerns, what Giussani and John Paul II call the "original," "primordial," "fundamental," or "constitutive" desires of the human heart. The realization that we share these concerns became the basis for a true friendship among us.

Among those present at these meetings was an editor at *The New York Times*. She invited me to write a column about my experiences as a confessor. The response to it was so positive that I received invitations to write books from the major secular publishing houses, as well as the invitation from *The New York Times* to be a regular contributor to their magazine. This led to the creation of the column "Intimations."

At the original dinner organized by my friend to introduce me to his New York colleagues, I met the TV producer, writer, and director Helen Whitney, who was working on a documentary for PBS-TV's program *Frontline* about the cultural challenges posed by the teachings and personality of Pope John Paul II. Helen invited me to be an official consultant for the program, and this opened the door to still another part of that world. My task was to "explain" to Helen some of the pope's most controversial teachings and to make sure that these were represented fairly in the show.

"The Millennial Pope" won many awards and as a result, I entered into conversation with PBS about the possibility of a new program that would discuss these issues on a weekly basis. Although the events of September 11 interrupted the fundraising for this effort, Helen was asked to do another show for *Frontline* dedicated precisely to September 11 and its religious implications. Again, I was asked to be the main consultant for this documentary, which was aired on the first anniversary of the terrorist attack with the title "Faith and Doubt at Ground Zero." The response to this effort was overwhelmingly favorable, and indeed in some cases deeply moving.

One fruit of these efforts was my book *God at the Ritz*, the result of the intense questioning on matters of religion and faith to which I was subjected during the presentation of the first *Frontline* program to the nation's media critics at their annual gathering in California to preview the new TV season. The book shows the approach I have been following in all of these efforts.

These experiences have shaped my understanding of the possibility of sharing the religious proposal in a secular context. First of all, I am convinced that there is at this time an opening for the religious proposal in these circles that was not there before. Most of the people I have met are aware of the failure of radical secularism to deal adequately with the big questions about human life and its meaning, both individually and socially. The inability of secularism to prevent the horrors of violence and death brought about by the great ideological monsters who sought to dominate the world in the twentieth century has shaken their confidence in the policy of relegating faith and religion to the purely private realm. As a result, the dominant ideology in those circles has become the "ideology of ambiguity," treasured as freedom's only defense against intolerance. Still, I believe that deep down most of them sense that this is not a solution, that this ambiguity soon leads to apathy and cynicism.

The mechanism by which this radical ambiguity is sustained is what Giussani called the "reduction of desire." There is a recognition that a truly human life demands more, that the human heart has an unquenchable desire for certainty and truth, and even that these cannot be found in ways of thinking that exclude the religious dimension. Without it, truth becomes the convictions of the most powerful. Secularists also sense that an ethics not based on a perception of the truth remains an artificial moralism—a moralism incapable of inspiring or moving anyone to great acts of creativity.

Still, secularists are afraid. In a sense, they are afraid to desire and expect too much. Why? Because this necessarily leads to religion, and they are terrified of the intolerance and violence that religion has often fostered. September 11 only intensified those fears. The popularity of "religion without truth claims" offers an escape for many people in our society today, but my friends in the media are too smart for that.

Those of us concerned with religion and the public square must address this concern. Two areas, I believe, are the most important.

The first is religion and reason—or better, religion and rationality. In a way, the religious question is secondary. It cannot be addressed adequately until an adequate view of rationality is developed, one based on experience and not on abstract arguments. Here experience means those "original" or "primordial" desires of the human heart and their implications. It is these implications—these ineradicable desires that constitute our humanity—that will open the door to the religious proposal.

In dialogues structured around these issues, it is important to demonstrate that religious believers share the same fundamental desires as those who are afraid of religion, and there is no stronger demonstration of this than the friendship offered and shown to our partners in dialogue. There is no need to hold back or disguise our convictions or to try to formulate a compromise or to look for a minimal "common ground." One editor of *The New York Times* told me: "Monsignor, we have many friends who are priests and who agree with us on almost everything. As a result, what they have to say is not really interesting. Those who disagree with us, however, do not want to be our friends. You are here because you do not agree with us on many issues, but it is obvious that you like us and see us as your friend."

The second area for study and dialogue is the relation between faith and tolerance. Does faith, with its absolutist connotations, necessarily lead to intolerance of different viewpoints? A faith limited to private conditions or feelings is not a threat, but then neither does it have any power to move anyone and play a serious role in culture.

Here the problem lies with the nature of "truth-claims" themselves. If these are taken seriously (as faith takes them), they appear to be incompatible with the requirements of a pluralistic society. As Joseph Cardinal Ratzinger (the future Pope Benedict XVI) wrote in an Italian journal of atheist thought—yes, Cardinal Ratzinger!—the greatest objection to religious thought today is its claim to be the only way to deal with ultimate issues. This concern was the heart of the pagan opposition to Christianity in the Roman Empire. Its position was perfectly summarized by a pagan author: "It is impossible to arrive at such a great mystery by only one way." Ratzinger comments, "The ethos of tolerance belongs to whoever recognizes in each way at best a part of the truth, to the one who does not place his own perception of it above any other and thus inserts himself serenely in the polymorphous symphony of the Inaccessible Eternal," or as someone told me during such a dialogue, the Unknowable Essence."

The most important problem to be dealt with in order to respond to the opening toward the religious sense that exists in those who experience the poverty of radical secularism is the relation between religion, reason, truth, and tolerance.

Tenderness and the Gas Chambers

The Challenges Facing Medicine Today

WALKER PERCY'S 1987 NOVEL *The Thanatos Syndrome*—his last one—tells the story of a psychiatrist who discovers that the government is conducting illegal mood-altering experiments on the unsuspecting population of a small town in order to eliminate violent crimes. The time of the action is in a near future in which abortion and euthanasia have become common practice in the medical profession. Dwelling in the same place is an old priest, considered an eccentric because he refuses to live in a parish and minister there. Instead, he lives on top of a tower used to spot forest fires. In one conversation with the psychiatrist, the priest tells him of his refusal to preach. It is useless, he says, because words have been deprived of their meaning.

Words convey experiences of life, experiences of our relation to nature, to the world and to others. Most importantly, words express our experience of the cosmos, that is, of the universe as a whole, of reality. Language expresses our relationship, our attitude, our stand with respect to the reality we experience. That is why certain words or expressions should not be translated literally, for they would not make any sense.

Take, for example, the expression "I'll buy that" to indicate agreement with what someone says. To my knowledge, there is no language other than English in which "buying" is synonymous with "agreeing." This tells us that those who use this expression experience the exchange of ideas and information in commercial categories like buying and selling. Life is somehow experienced as one great commercial enterprise. When you translate "I'll buy that" into another language, you'll have to simply say "I agree" in that language, but something has been lost in the translation of your experience of reality.

Words, then, are signs, symbols, that convey much more than information. They convey personal experiences. To grow up speaking a given language is to experience life as those people who speak that language experience it. When you use words, therefore, you are communicating much more than your own experience, you are communicating the most fundamental and profound experience of an entire people. That is why, even when a word is exactly the same in two languages, and even when it has the same dictionary meaning, the word may convey false information—because the experiences and attitude toward reality of the two persons speaking are different.

For example, "yes" and "no" do not mean the same to an Anglo and a Hispanic person. When an Anglo wants to say no to someone's proposal, he or she will just say "no." The Hispanic is different. There are many situations when to say "no" bluntly may be considered insulting to the other person, disrespectful, especially if it is someone with whom you have a close relationship. Therefore the Hispanic will say "yes" while having no intention of going along with what is proposed. Yet this is not lying! Another Hispanic will know, deep inside, that the "yes" may still mean "no," because the other Hispanic shares the same fundamental presupposition about interpersonal relations. This example was once used by the Archbishop of Miami in a talk to Anglo pastors angry with their Hispanic parishioners because they had agreed to do something and then did not do it. These same pastors also wondered what they had done to offend some parishioners to whom they said "no" without any intention of giving offense.

Words, therefore, will signify adequately when there is a common tradition of experiences between those who are speaking. In *The Thanatos Syndrome* the old priest says that he no longer preaches because the most important words about life have been deprived of the experiences of the tradition that gave rise to them and are now used to convey other experiences, experiences contrary even to the original ones behind the words. Words no longer signify what they once did, he holds.

Let me give you an example. A preacher might say, invoking the great spiritual masters of the Catholic tradition, that you cannot know God unless you know yourself, because God is present in the deepest part of yourself. This is what the word "interiority" means in spiritual theology: God is interior to us. Yet I suggest to you that a preacher who says this today will be understood in a way totally opposite to what "interiority" and knowledge of self meant to the great Catholic masters of spirituality. Why? Because the modern way of thinking has *secularized* interiority. It has made it a *psychological* concept, not a spiritual one. The reduction of spirituality to psychology is one of the main reasons why the traditional words of Catholic doctrine no longer signify what they once did. If they are used, they will not only not signify adequately what the tradition meant, but they will actually lead us away from what the tradition meant.

Modern psychology developed in a culture that rejected the transcendent dimension of human existence, that is, the relation between a human being and a God that is totally beyond what we can think, imagine, or desire—the God who lives in "unapproachable light" and can only be approached if he gives us the capacity as a gift, a grace which in no way depends on our powers to accomplish what it does accomplish. The modern world rejected that and made the human being and human capacities and needs the sole measure of what is real. Modern psychology has its roots in that rejection. The results of all its experiments and its speculations are necessarily affected by that rejection; they are the fruits of that prejudice. They are not objective scientific results; they are prejudiced results.

When modern psychology insists on our need to know ourselves, it does not mean what, say, Saint Augustine meant. For Saint Augustine, knowing oneself is knowing as God knows us, as created by God, as existing because of the free decision of a transcendent God. But by this same phrase modern psychology means knowing ourselves precisely as the authors of our individual existence, as the makers of our own identity. The father of the modern age, René Descartes, said: "I know, therefore I am." Joseph Ratzinger says that the Christian claim is different; it is "I *am known*, therefore I am" (known, of course, by the God who created me and sustains me in existence). The phrase "know yourself," therefore, has been secularized; it has been deprived of the depth it once had; it has been deprived of its meaning.

Percy calls this the "evacuation of the sign."

Now it is this evacuation of the sign which, according to the priest, lies behind the medical profession's willingness to perform abortions and practice euthanasia, all in the name of compassion or tenderness. What has made this possible is the secularization of the word "tenderness." Tenderness has been deprived of its meaning. The word no longer communicates the experience of transcendence that it once conveyed.

The old priest in *The Thanatos Syndrome* asks the psychiatrist to play a word free-association game with him. The words chosen are: "clouds, Irish, Black, and Jews." With clouds the psychiatrist associates "sky, fleecy, puffy, floating, and white." With Irish he associates "Bogs, Notre Dame," and the generic name "Pat O'Brien." With Black it is words like "Africa, minority. . . civil rights." In each case the psychiatrist has replied with concepts, ideas, descriptions, general terms that apply to many things in addition to the given word.

But with "Jews," it is different. With "Jews" the psychiatrist mostly associates the names of concrete Jews that he knows or has known, concrete persons. The priest says: "What you associated with the word-sign Irish were certain connotations, stereotypical Irish stuff in your head. Same for Black. If I had said Spanish, you'd have said something like guitars, castanets, bullfights, and such." These words have been evacuated because they no longer mean something real and concrete. They designate *abstractions* that apply to many examples.

In the case of "Jews," however, the vast majority of associations were concrete persons that really existed. The word "Jew," the priest says, cannot be deprived of its meaning. It cannot be made abstract, theoretical. The reason is that the one thing that defines Jews is that divine intervention that made them—and just them—the chosen people. This is the only reason Jews are distinct, absolutely distinct, from anyone else: their existence, their identity comes from God's free, unmerited, sovereign decision, inexplicable in human terms. There is absolutely nothing in the Jews that made them the chosen people; it was God's free decision. Indeed, without this divine election, there would be no Jews. Indeed, even Jews who do not believe in God still consider themselves Jews. A transcendent God is the guarantor of Jewish existence and identity. Jews exist as a sign of transcendence and nothing else.

What happens to Jews, then, in a world where the experience of transcendence has been rejected, suppressed, and even lost? In that world, Jews stand out as an unbearable singularity. The priest says: "This [singularity] offends people, even the most talented people,

people of the loftiest sentiments, the highest scientific achievements and the purest humanitarian ideals." The reason is that such people have fallen victims to abstract, theorizing, generalizing thinking, the sort of thinking science needs to express its universal theories that are then placed at the service of technology in order to improve human life.

Since science and technology require abstract thought, the culture created by science and technology, such as ours, cannot tolerate the singular, the concrete, the unrepeatable. It cannot tolerate the truly personal. It cannot even see it. That is why it cannot see anything wrong with abortion or euthanasia. It cannot see personhood in the womb; it cannot see personhood in the sick and aged that no longer function or perform acts that fit their theories of authentic human behavior. For that way of thinking, human imperfections and suffering are useless; they are not mysteries pointing to transcendence; they are problems to be solved, malfunctions. And when they cannot be solved or fixed, those who are in this condition cease to be human as science and technology defines the human, and therefore they are discarded as one discards the totally useless. Their existence is seen, even experienced, as a painful and sad failure, and so they are put away in the name of compassion or tenderness. That is why, in such a world of secularized interiority, our modern world, tenderness leads to the gas chambers.

Percy's words here are so magnificent that I want you to hear exactly how the priest explains this:

> You are a member of the first generation of doctors in the history of medicine to turn their backs on the oath of Hippocrates and kill millions of old, useless people, unborn children, born malformed children, for the good of mankind—and to do so without a single murmur from one of you. Not a single letter of protest in the august *New England Journal of Medicine*. And do you know what you are going to end up doing? You a graduate of Harvard and a reader of *The New York Times* and a member of the Ford Foundation's Program for the Third World? Do you know what is going to happen to you? You are going to end up killing Jews....
>
> If you are a lover of Mankind in the abstract like Walt Whitman, who wished the best for Mankind, you will probably do no harm and might even write good poetry and give pleasure....

If you are a theorist of mankind like Rousseau or Skinner, who believes he understands Man's brain and in the solitariness of his study or laboratory writes books on the subject, you are also probably harmless and might even contribute to human knowledge. . . .

But if you put the two together, a lover of Mankind and a Theorist of Mankind, what you've got now is Robespierre or Stalin or Hitler and the Terror, and millions dead for the good of Mankind.

And at the end of the book, in a homily to the medical community engaging in the experiments with drugs to eliminate violent crime he says:

Never in the history of the world have there been so many civilized tenderhearted souls as have lived in this century. Never in the history of the world have so many people been killed. More people have been killed in this century by tenderhearted souls than by cruel barbarians in all other centuries put together. . . . My brothers, let me tell you where tenderness leads. . . . Tenderness leads to the gas chambers.

For all Catholic medical professionals, Walker Percy, who is now in eternity, offers an important lesson. Twenty years before, the novelist Flannery O'Connor had made the same point almost in the exact same words. But since she was writing an essay and not a novel, and an essay as a Catholic, she was able to go to the very roots of the problem as our Catholic faith reveals it. O'Connor was writing an introduction to the story of a twelve-year-old girl who had died of a disfiguring facial cancer after years of being an inspiration to the care-givers and other patients in the facility where she lived. O'Connor was arguing that today many people would see no meaning to this girl's life. She would be a "problem" that could not be solved by science and technology, and therefore the fullness of her humanity would not be appreciated by those whose way of thinking corresponded to the scientific, technical, abstracting, theorizing, problem-solving way.

And so she wrote that those people, in order to "cut down human imperfection," would be destroying that which our faith tells us is the "raw material for good" (since our faith sees human suffering as capable of bearing tremendous spiritual fruit). "In this popular pity," she says, "we mark our gain in sensibility but our loss in vision. If other ages felt less, they saw more, even though they saw with the blind, prophetical, unsentimental eye of acceptance which is to say of faith. In this absence of faith now, we govern by tenderness. It is a tenderness which, long since cut off from the person of Christ, is wrapped in theory. When tenderness is detached from the source of tenderness, its logical outcome is terror. It ends in forced labor camps and in the fumes of the gas chambers."

Now we are at the heart of the problem. Notice what she says: the source of tenderness is the person of Christ. Otherwise, it is wrapped in theory, and theory cannot include what is unique, singular, concrete, and unrepeatable. Theory cannot deal with persons. Theory can deal with "the poor," but not with that unique poor person. Theory can deal with "the suffering," but not with that unique suffering person. Theory can deal with "the sick," but not with that unique sick person. Theory cannot grasp the singular; it reduces all to one common denominator so that it can derive laws of behavior, statistics, and programs of action that deal with problems to be solved, not with persons to be loved. Each single human person is unique and unrepeatable because of his or her interiority, because of his or her transcendence, because of the roots of personal identity in a God who is absolutely beyond what this world could ever imagine or reach with its powers and techniques. A culture where transcendence has been rejected is a deadly culture for persons.

This, I propose to you, is the culture in which we live right now. It is, as John Paul II said bluntly in 1993 at World Youth Day in Denver, a "culture of death." And it is this culture in which doctors and nurses must exercise their vocations as healers. Learn well, then, what Flannery O'Connor saw so clearly: the only remedy against theory is the person of Jesus Christ, since he and he alone is the one from whom our transcendence as persons comes. We are persons because he became one of us. He is the Chosen One of God. He is Israel. He is all Jews. And in him, we become Israel, we are chosen, and as such, our existence comes from beyond this world and therefore cannot be subject to the calculations and standards of this world.

This insight must be at the heart of the work of the Catholic medical professional. Many Catholics have lost the experiences of the Catholic tradition behind such words as justice, love, sin, eternity, suffering, and compassion—and tenderness itself. Their Catholic faith has become another abstraction, another theory. That is why Pope John Paul II called for a New Evangelization: to restore to us those experiences. These experiences can be found only in that life of personal union with Jesus Christ that is the life of the Church. Having lost these experiences, the Church, and even the Person of Christ himself, have become empty symbols, abstractions, inspirational concepts, ways of acquiring moral values.

Insofar as Catholic medical professionals come together to support each other, they ought to avoid becoming a circle for ethical or inspirational discussions. This would be deadly; it would fall right into the hands of the dominant anti-Christian and anti-human culture that has killed and is killing millions through medical knowledge. The Catholic doctor ought to beware of a fascination with medico-moral issues detached from the only context in which they can be discussed without harm, namely the context of a living experience of the following of Jesus Christ.

This is the most important teaching of John Paul II's encyclical *Veritatis Splendor*, which makes it clear that the moral life is lived in the following of Jesus Christ, the *sequela Christi*. Moral reasoning takes place in a dialogue with Jesus Christ such as that of the rich young man upon which *Veritatis Splendor* is based. That is why another important source for reflection is the *Catechism of the Catholic Church*. When the Catechism was first released in Europe, secular observers were amazed by its serenity, its concreteness, its attractive confidence that God has indeed entered this world in Jesus Christ and that it is possible to experience this presence and come into contact with it with all our faculties, including our senses. The appearance of Jesus Christ is an event, a reality that happens, and Christians are those to whom this has happened, such that they have seen and believed. The gospel is about this real event offered to us; it is not about moral theories, values, and problems to be solved.

Finally, to the extent that Catholic medical professionals come together to support each other in their paths, those moments must provide the opportunity for them to experience the life of the Church as friends and companions brought together in solidarity, in communion, in that being-together without which it is absolutely impossible to be a follower of Jesus Christ. Such gatherings either offer the opportunity to experience the life of the Church together—to truly experience the

Catholic faith as a way of life, as an experience of reality—or they are a waste of time, because they will not address the origin of our unrest, our need to be together. All must flow from the experience of mass and the sacraments, celebrated together, lived together, experienced together. Without this, everything else will be deprived of a contact with reality and thus easily domesticated and put at the service of the dominant modern mentality that has led to the "culture of death."

I commend you to the protection and intercession of Mary, the Mother of the Eternal Son of God, in whose womb He became flesh: her flesh, our flesh.

On Being a Witness

The Catholic Lawyer and the Method of Presence

WHEN WE THINK ABOUT the relationship between faith and work, the first thing that comes to our minds is the ethical perspective that our faith contributes to society. But this is not what defines Catholic professionals as Catholic. In fact, if our ethics were to be the test of our identity as Catholics, I fear most of us would have to abandon the claim. What defines us as Catholics—what defines us as Christians, as followers of Christ—is not our moral behavior; it is not anything that originates in our efforts.

Let me give you an example. I have a friend in Italy who is a crook, a thief. He is retired now, but on occasion he works as a consultant (an expensive one at that) with stores seeking to update their security systems. He really was an excellent crook. No jewelry store was safe from his exceptional talent.

On one occasion, though, he was unable to do his work. He and his companions were already inside this store when suddenly he saw an image of the Blessed Virgin Mary. He immediately cancelled the robbery. His accomplices were amazed. "Are you afraid of a statue," they asked him? "No," he said. "It's the Blessed Virgin, *la Madonna*, my mother. How can I be afraid of her?" "Then why are you calling off the job?" they asked. He explained, "Because tomorrow, when the robbery is discovered, people will say she was unable to protect them." And so they went and robbed another store.

There is no question that my friend is a Christian—a Catholic, in fact. He may be a sinner, a crook, but he is a Catholic sinner, a Catholic crook.

Compare this case to someone who would never steal because he thinks stealing is wrong. Is he a Christian? If the fact that he thinks it is wrong to steal is all we know about him, then we cannot tell whether he is a Christian or not. If he has the strength to overcome temptations to do something wrong, we do not know whether he is a Catholic or not. Remember that the only person in the Bible of whom it is explicitly said that he had observed all the commandments, that rich young man who asked Christ what to do to gain eternal life, decided not to follow Jesus. And in the parable of the Pharisee and the Publican, the Pharisee thanks God for being able to observe the moral law, and yet Jesus says he was not justified, whereas the Publican sinner was.

When Saint Augustine in *The City of God* is trying to identify what distinguishes its citizens from the citizens of the "earthly city"— what distinguishes Christians from non-Christians—he recognizes that the dividing line, so to speak, is not in the area of moral behavior. As he says, we know that so many times non-Christians are equally if not more ethically-motivated than Christians. For Saint Augustine, what distinguishes Christians from non-Christians is an event—that is, something that has happened to us that has not happened to those who do not know Christ.

As a result of this event, we see everything around us in a manner different from those to whom the event has not occurred. More precisely, as a result of what happened, our hope for the satisfaction of those desires for happiness that define the human heart is different from the hope of those to whom the event has not occurred.

A Catholic lawyer is a lawyer, an expert in law, as good or bad as determined by the standards of his or her profession, as ethical or unethical as his or her formation and inner moral strength allows—a lawyer like any other—but one to whom something has happened that has not happened to the others. And as a result that something has changed the reasons for his or her hopes.

According to Augustine, the hope of the Christian is placed entirely "on the grace and mercy of the true God." Non-Christians lack this hope, not because they are sinners (Christians are sinners too, otherwise they would not have experienced mercy!), but because they have not had the experience of the events that makes the presence of Jesus Christ a decisive factor in their lives, the factor that determines how they see and experience human life.

These events, remember, are not the outcome of our efforts or programs of ethical, psychological, or religious renewal. They are not the result of our spirituality. They are factual, objective events that occur to us as something unforeseen, unimaginable, an undeserved gift, a grace. The Christian is the one who can say with Saint Thérèse, "Everything is grace." Everything is mercy; everything is the fruit of an unmerited and unconditional love. Everything, every single aspect of life, everything that exists, is the manifestation of this grace and mercy. Grace and mercy are the truth of all of reality. And all the circumstances of our lives—including our sins, including our sufferings—occur so that we can recognize the grace and mercy of the presence of Christ in reality. As Saint Paul writes, "Christ is all and in all" (Col 3:11).

It is important to underline that the hope that defines the Christian is not merely limited to life in heaven or to the end of the world. The hope of the Christian is based on the grace and mercy revealed in this life, in this world, revealed through concrete events that take place in this world. It is a hope, therefore, that concerns what happens and what has happened and what could happen in this world, in this life. It is a conviction of what is possible in this life and of the way that what is possible can actually happen: it can happen not because of what our efforts and talents and intelligence make possible, but because of the events that make Christ present in this world.

Let me give you an example. Few people understood the way Pope John Paul II saw the war in Iraq and why he was so concerned, urging all involved to do everything possible to avoid it. The pope was not a pacifist. Those who appealed to his opposition to the war to justify their pacifism or their political preferences were manipulating his words. He was not saying that the war was immoral, that it was sinful, or that Catholic soldiers should not fight in it. John Paul II was a realist. He knew that in the human efforts to struggle against injustice, to defend human dignity and protect our freedom, war may be necessary. He knew and appreciated the American people's love for freedom and the sacrifices made to help other people struggle for it. He knew that without these sacrifices, Nazism and Communism would have continued to enslave his own country.

Taking as a point of departure what can be achieved with our efforts and resources, including our moral sensibilities and ethical judgments, I have no doubt that the pope was sympathetic to the American arguments for the war, although, of course, he could not say so publicly. As Saint Augustine wrote, the citizens of the City of God—the followers of Christ—recognize the efforts for justice and peace by the citizens of the earthly city and will discharge their civic responsibilities when ordered to do so by the legitimate authority. In their hearts, though, they recognize that the best of these efforts will prove insufficient to bring about the desired justice, peace, and freedom. Only the grace of Christ can set us free. Their hope is based not on human effort, but on the power of Christ's victory, the victory of grace and mercy over what enslaves us as a result of our sins.

To be the witness of this grace and peace made possible by Christ is the greatest contribution that the Christian citizen can make to his society's quest for justice, peace, and freedom. War may be necessary, even ethically just, but it cannot be considered as the means to achieve what the human heart desires and needs. War, even if reasonable from the perspective of what is possible by our efforts, always involves a defeat for man because it cannot secure the peace, justice, and freedom that we need and instead opens the door to grave dangers. This is what the pope was saying, accompanied by the call for prayers that the grace and mercy of Christ might bring the peace and freedom that we need.

The greatest contribution the Catholic lawyer can make in his professional world is to live and work in a way that gives witness to the grace and mercy without which true justice will never be found. Without this true justice, Saint Augustine said, "What are governments if not bands of robbers?"

Catholic lawyers serve this justice through their work by being witnesses to the power of the grace and mercy that they have experienced through their encounter with Christ and the events of his life that brought about our salvation. It is a matter of the way we are present in our professional world. The presence of the Catholic lawyer in the world of human laws opens up that world to the new possibilities revealed by grace and mercy.

The Christian's presence in the world must not be what Giussani calls a "reactive" presence. A reactive presence is one shaped by ideas and expectations that do not take into account the power of the grace of Christ to open up possibilities that exceed what we can bring about by our best thinking and our strongest efforts. To be reactive is to play in a game whose rules are determined by those who have not met Christ. When we do this, we are ignoring Christ's presence in the world and therefore our vision of what is real and its possibilities is flawed. We are reacting to what is there, instead of generating new possibilities, accepting the limited hopes of a world without Christ, instead of generating a new hope.

Another temptation to be avoided is that of being moved by utopian thinking. A utopia is the vision of a situation supposed to prevail in the future, a situation whose image and scheme of values are created by us, to be brought about by our projects and plans—a cultural project. Saint Thomas More, the patron of lawyers, wrote a book called *Utopia*. And yet, when reality caught up with him, he did not find the strength to confront the injustice of his conviction and sentence by reflecting on an imagined future. Instead, he made it very clear that he recognized that he was being persecuted because of his fidelity to Christ, his fidelity to the presence of Christ in the world through the Church founded on the apostles in communion with Peter. This is what made him a martyr, that is, a witness. He was a good citizen of England. He accepted the authority of the king and was willing to help him with his considerable intelligence. He would not work for nor seek exile in a country other than England. And yet he was willing to die to defend the liberty and authority of the Church—that is, the reality of the Church as the bearer of the hopes and possibilities for freedom and justice in this world—not because all the leaders and members of the Church were paragons of virtue and fidelity, but because the origin of the Church was the event of Christ's presence, an event of grace and mercy. This is the witness that the Catholic lawyer is called to offer today.

The Catholic lawyer is a lawyer whose identity is defined by his or her belonging to Christ. It is this identity-as-belonging that generates the way he or she is present in the world. The presence that originates in this belonging generates hope, that is, a new awareness of what is possible in our quest for justice. It is an awareness expressed in a new way of being human, the beginning of the new world brought about by Christ's victory over sin and death, that is, the new world created entirely by grace and mercy.

This new way of being human is characterized by an exceptional recognition of the dignity of our humanity because it is through humanity that God revealed himself as grace and mercy. This is the guiding concern of the Catholic lawyer. The Catholic lawyer will use all of his or her legal talents to give witness to this dignity.

And here Giussani's emphasis on the "method of presence" as opposed to utopia is key. The utopian way of thinking expresses itself through "speech, projects, and the anxious search for instruments and organizational forms." The "method of presence," on the other hand, has as its expression an "operative friendship" for concrete human persons, resulting in a different way of being a protagonist in human history, "enter[ing] into everything, mak[ing] use of everything" through gestures of real humanity, that is, of charity, in order to give witness to this dignity.

Some lawyers initially motivated by utopian thinking end up by cynically accepting the imperfections and corruption that they see all around them. The more they try to change things, the stronger the opposition seems to be. Those that do not give in suffer great frustrations. When I asked a few Catholic lawyers to tell me what their Catholic identity meant to them, all of them spoke first of the suffering it brought them as they struggled to promote and defend real justice. They were frequently tempted to give up, to do what all the others do and give in to "the system." But if they did, they felt guilty and wished they had pursued another path instead of the legal profession.

The choice of presence over utopia is different. This means building the future not on what we dream about, but on what has already happened, on what the presence of Christ means for this world. This is the basis for our realism, not what we think can be, but what already is, because of Christ. That is why we are not discouraged, no matter what the situations in which we find ourselves. Our task is not to build a future; it is to give witness, to plant the seeds of a future that is already present in Christ, that is being built by the power of his presence. The future is already within this seed. It will come to the surface in its own time, "as we wait in joyful hope for the coming of Our Savior Jesus Christ."

Because this future is already in our midst, the Catholic lawyer believes that what happened to him or to her, the event that became real to him or to her, can just as easily become real for the legally guilty person that the lawyer defends or prosecutes. Indeed, there are many cases of prisoners to whom this has happened while in jail. The just laws of the state must be enforced in such a way that the dignity of the humanity of even the most heinous criminal is respected because the kingdom of God, the city of God, the share in God's own life, is as close to him as it was to us when we recognized it as pure gift, an undeserved grace. At no time, therefore, will the Catholic lawyer be motivated by a desire for revenge, either on behalf of the state or his or her clients.

The key to the mission of the Catholic lawyer is thus to express our identity as belonging to Christ in all the circumstances of our lives, to categorically reject the limitation of the consequences of this identity to the private, inner sphere. It is a matter of avoiding being a Catholic and a lawyer in favor of being a lawyer who is a Catholic. The Catholic lawyer is one who refuses to separate his identity from his life as a lawyer not only in terms of values and ethics, but in the way everything is viewed, approached, judged, and lived. The purpose of every action is the presence of what we are. All the rest follows from this.

Joseph Ratzinger said that today's man is a man for whom Christianity is a past that does not concern him. And already in the 1930s, Charles Péguy noticed that the modern world is the first world since the coming of Christ in which Christ is not present as the decisive factor in our lives. The world today may respect the memory of Christ (although even this seems to be waning), and it may have a high opinion of the ethical teachings of Christ, of the social importance of Christian values, but Jesus Christ as such—his real and concrete presence as a protagonist and factor of life—does not concern the modern world.

Lawyers are among the most influential people in the world today. Since Christ is absent, everything seems to depend on the laws for their own sake, laws in which procedure prevails over reality. What was a society governed by laws that reflected the real has become a society enslaved by legalism.

So in a sense, it is an awesome time to be a Catholic lawyer. It means having the opportunity to be the embodiment of the presence that will break through this stifling and enslaving legalism and return reality to the law and thus contribute to the salvation of this world—and all entirely because of grace and mercy and the hope coming from it that is capable of changing the human heart.

Tending Toward the One

The University and the Evangelization of Culture

CULTURE MAY BE DESCRIBED as the way a people's experiences are shaped by a defining stance before reality. It relates each moment to an ultimate horizon of perception and action, both individual and corporate. Culture is guided by a judgment about the totality of the real, recognized explicitly or assumed implicitly. We may say that culture is an expression of reason—that is, our capacity to reach judgments about the meaning of particular experiences by linking them to a larger whole. So, in a deeper sense, culture is an expression of what might be called the "religious sense," the human impulse to relate the particular to the total in order to discover the ultimate sense or meaning of individual experiences.

The evangelization of culture can only occur through an education of the religious sense. A culture is evangelized when the rationality that guides it is the result of an encounter with the Risen Christ. If culture is based on an experience of a reality judged rationally, evangelization occurs when Jesus Christ is recognized—affirmed to be, critically judged to be—*that* reality.

The evangelization of culture therefore does not take place by introducing the Christian message as a discourse—a lingo or set of ideas—no matter how correctly formulated or articulate. This type of evangelization cannot change the culture because a discourse is already at a remove from the originating experiences of reality that generated it. Any discourse introduced into a culture will be interpreted in terms of its preconceptions about reality. Evangelization can only occur through methods that overcome reductionist, ideological preconceptions. It occurs when the encounter with Christ is recognized as corresponding to those demands of the human person that propel the religious sense.

This is all the more so in our present cultural landscape. Although the influence of the Protestant faith in this country has slowed the process somewhat, our intellectual culture is still moving with Western Europe toward that point described by Nietzsche: "Facts no longer exist; only interpretations." This observation is echoed by Hannah Arendt:

> The most disconcerting and surprising aspect of the flight from reality is the habit of treating facts as if they were mere opinions. [Thus] all facts can be changed, all lies can be made to be true. . . . What we are struggling against is not the result of indoctrination as much as it is the incapacity or the lack of disposition to distinguish between facts and opinions. As a result many can agree with Malraux's observation: "There is no ideal for which we can sacrifice, because we know the lie in all of them, we who do not know what truth is."

Obviously, such a culture cannot be evangelized through a mere intellectual proposal. As soon as that proposal is exposed to the dominant culture, it will be reduced to one more interpretation or opinion.

The university is by its very nature a place to overcome this type of nihilism. The very word testifies to it: *uni-versitas*. The university is a place where the many aspects of the human quest for knowledge tend toward (*vertere, versus*) an *unum* that brings together the university as a community of learning and gives sense and purpose to the quest for knowledge at all levels. It is this "tending toward" that defines a true university and distinguishes it from a training center at the service of the ruling powers. It is the basis of respect for "academic freedom" itself.

The university's greatest contribution to the evangelization of culture is to open the culture to the experience of the event of Christ as the beckoning *unum* that gives consistency to reality and that sustains and promotes the *curiositas* that drives the human quest for understanding. Our task is not to somehow integrate a technological culture with a humanistic culture by adding ethical and social values to the cold logic of a calculating mentality. What is at stake is the very possibility of an experience of true knowledge whose confines, so to speak, will never be closed, since the quest for "meaning" constitutes the very motor of learning as the measure of a truly human education.

Instead, today we face a situation in which education is conceived as the self-acquisition of abstract and formal competences. In this new understanding of education, the student can proceed without experiencing the "tending towards the *unum*" of a tradition of meaning personified in a teacher and offered to the student's freedom for verification by comparison with the defining nature of the human heart.

The human taste for research is neither born nor sustained by this reductionist view of education. Rather, the love for research is born when, in our relation with things and with other persons, we are confronted with the hypothesis that all of this has meaning. Without this encounter—when education is just methodology without content—the very possibility of discovering something truly new is eliminated and we remain at the mercy of ideologies that pretend to explain everything through their preconceptions.

In his poem *Choruses From The Rock*, T.S. Eliot asks: "Where is the Life we have lost in living? / Where is the wisdom we have lost in knowledge? / Where is the knowledge we have lost in information?" And later in the poem he asks: "Has the Church failed mankind or has mankind failed the Church?"

I am tempted to ask: has the university failed mankind or has mankind failed the university? The answers to these questions are inseparable. From its very origin, the university is linked to the life of the Church. One of the ways the Church helps mankind is through the university; one of the ways the Church fails mankind is through the university.

The Church fails mankind when the university ceases to be a place of encounter with Christ as the center of history and the universe—not as a theological proposition, but an event that discloses the full meaning of reality. (As Giussani says, we can adhere to the theological proposition that Jesus Christ is the center of history and the universe, and that certainly is the truth. But before he was that, Christ was a lump of blood in the womb of a young Jewish woman.)

An encounter with Christ, the encounter that changes the way we look at reality—because it is a fact, not a proposition, an experience, not an intellectual proposal—is an encounter with a concrete human individual of flesh and blood. The encounter that generates a new cultural proposal with the capacity to break through the ideology of interpretations must be an encounter with human flesh and blood.

The Church evangelizes culture by being the place of such an encounter, and the Catholic university evangelizes culture by being a place where the life of the Church is experienced as an opening to the totality of reality. If the Catholic university fails to be a place for the evangelization of culture, it is because the life of the Church—of which the Catholic university is an expression—is not perceived as the human space of the presence of the risen Christ, and as such, the living experience of the meaning of human life.

The victory of Christ over the destruction of humanity is the creation of the Church as a people, as a way of coming together to live the life made possible by the paschal mystery, to be the body of the risen Christ, that is, as a human realization of his salvation of history through a love stronger than all the evil in the world. Christians live as witnesses to the goodness of reality, with a hope that "does not disappoint" (Rom 5:5), that moves us to pursue with passion the quest for knowledge of reality in all its dimensions, including its roots in creation, certain that the assurance of the fulfillment of our mortal condition is a real possibility in this life.

When this experience is lost, Christianity ceases to be the experience of an event, of a fact, and instead becomes a utopia, an ideology, an abstract discourse, and thus completely unable to change a culture that imprisons us in a war of interpretations and exposes us to the power of those with the ability and resources to make their interpretations prevail.

The evangelization of culture will not occur until the originating experience of the Christian people is retrieved. Then the Catholic university would be a privileged means for this mission, simply by being a real university.

Risk, Investment, and Creativity

MY ONLY EXPERIENCE OF putting money into the market is my weekly trip to The Food Emporium, so I cannot even pretend to understand the insights, experiences, language, and methods that characterize the work of those in wealth management and investment. I am a Catholic priest who is a former aerospace physicist. My scientific background has given me a great appreciation for all human efforts to develop existing resources for human progress and to create new ones. My philosophical and theological studies have led me to consider this progress in light of the great questions in the human heart about the purpose and meaning of life, and my faith sustains the hope that the desires that propel such a quest will in the end prevail over all obstacles to human development. I offer here, then, some thoughts I hope will be helpful for those who are working in wealth management and the world of investment.

As a result of the recent financial scandals that have called into question the suitability and efficacy of the procedures designed to prevent corruption, many are calling for additional supervision and ethical reform of those involved in the financial sector. Realistic ethical principles, however, must originate in the human heart; otherwise we risk the danger of moralism and of a paralyzing—and ironically unjust—legalism. It is to this fundamental level that I would like to direct my attention.

I have in mind the level where the freedom that makes us human originates. The crucial importance of the work of the investor is understood and appreciated only by penetrating into this level of human life. Socialism and Marxism erred by not taking into account the fundamental human need for freedom. That is why they failed. The economics of the free market triumphed over them because it is open to the reality of freedom. In fact, it depends on it. When it doesn't, when it ignores freedom, when it is not rooted in the human experience of freedom, then it too leads to an inhuman way of life and brings about conflicts that tear societies apart.

Investments are an exercise of freedom. They are a form of risk, and risk is inseparable from freedom. Risk is based on a judgment that involves a decision. A decision is an act of freedom based on reason—based, that is, on evidence that brings about certainty.

At first impression, perhaps, it may not seem so. It may seem that risk is taken precisely when there is uncertainty. This may be the case with gambling, but not with the kind of risks associated with investment. This risk is born and sustained by a certainty sustained by evidence. Without certainty based on evidence, there is no freedom. It is just a matter of rules that are followed blindly, a matter of instinct having nothing to do with reason. Without evidence and certainty, the risk of investment is unreasonable. It has no meaning.

But what is this certainty like? Upon what evidence is it based? It is important to know this. If we want people to invest, it is important to know how this certainty is born, upon what evidence it is based, and how it is that it moves our freedom to take risks.

What separates freedom from enslavement is the existence of a nucleus in the individual person that cannot be entirely reduced to his or her bio-historical antecedents. The reality of this nucleus is based on experience, provided this has not been rendered impossible by fear or by cultural conditioning.

The experience in question is the experience of desire. These desires, or demands, or exigencies are profoundly united in their roots. They are characterized by the fact that they are structurally insatiable, that is, nothing can satisfy them fully. As such, they always point beyond, always beyond and beyond, towards infinity. Therefore, they always keep open the potential for great possibilities, creating an intuition that recognizes new beginnings as possible. It is the certainty that this is so, based on the evidence of the reality of those insatiable demands of the human heart, that moves our freedom to take risks for a better future.

This is why the work of investment is so important. It is not only a matter of increasing personal wealth or the social benefits that come from the economic expansion that such work helps bring about. It is a matter also of the link between this work and those desires of the human heart upon which our liberty depends. As such, I am not afraid to say, the work of an investor has a spiritual dimension.

Today there is talk about the need to bring together spirituality and work, and many corporations have developed programs for this purpose. But this is not what I have in mind. I don't think there is any need to add something called "spirituality" to work. I think all authentic work itself has a spiritual dimension, and its major importance lies in that.

By "spiritual" I do not mean an otherworldly reality. Spiritual designates a human reality, a human experience—namely, the experience of limitless desire. This could also be designated as the religious sense, understanding religion to designate not the revelation of a reality beyond this world, but a human orientation to infinity. My claim is that work—all truly human work—is a manifestation of the religious sense. Otherwise, it becomes alienating and destructive. This is especially true in the economic sphere, which depends entirely on human creativity.

Indeed, without this link to the human desire for infinity, the world of finance and economics becomes a struggle for raw power, for power as such, and this is ultimately the basis for its corruption. All power has the temptation to become independent of whatever threatens to limit it. It accomplishes this precisely by the reduction of desire, by extinguishing the infinite destiny to which the desires of the human heart point—that is, by destroying the basis for creativity. Power is threatened by creativity. That is why it fears authentic risks, creating an environment inimical to authentic human development. It is the same with the power of the state that wishes to entirely control the economy as it is with a corrupt economic power pursued for its own sake.

A market economy based on respect for the human openness to infinity will be rich in initiatives reflecting the possibilities of human creativity. Such an economic system will be in perfect accordance with human liberty.

It is clear that in such a case, investments will not be seen as a game of chance, as a gamble intended only to multiply personal riches without additional work. Instead, they will be seen as the extension of work itself.

Work is a necessity of the human person. It is not enough to con-sider it to be only a right, a duty, a factor of production, or an activity required for survival. This is not enough. Work is a necessity at the deepest level of human personhood, at the level of the openness to infinity revealed by the desires of the heart. It is a constitutive factor of human personal life, of the human being as such. Work is insepa-rable from liberty.

Work cannot be separated from the context of all those demands of the heart required for an authentically human life, such as friend-ship, play, contemplation of beauty, and so forth. To isolate work from these is to build the economic system on a distorted idea of what it means to be a human being, making it inherently unstable and sus-tained only by power. Again, the detachment of economic and political power from the original needs of the heart, from the religious sense, is the basis for corruption in politics and in the economic world, and no program of ethical reform based on abstract values will ever deal with it adequately.

All human activities that seek human personal development must be attentive to the totality of the person rather than restricting their scope to only those factors that deal with the production of riches and expansion of resources. The totality of the person must also be consid-ered when one speaks of the common good pursued by the leaders of a society. Only this will allow each one to be a true protagonist in social life by means of his or her creative initiatives, which always require risk. This risk, however, is readily taken precisely because it is made reasonable by the experience of being such a protagonist, by the expe-rience of the infinite scope of human desires and possibilities.

In the end, it is a matter of culture, of the difference between a cul-ture that promotes such initiatives and a culture that discourages them.

In an address to UNESCO, Pope John Paul II spoke of the exis-tence of a "primary" and a "secondary" culture. A primary culture is based on the cultivation of resources (the word culture comes from the word "cultivate") in order to promote this orientation to infinity that points to a destiny for each human being. A secondary culture is based on the knowledge and use of all particular aspects that make up the specific area of life being cultivated. Expertise in investments creates a secondary culture that must be placed at the service of the primary culture in order to respond to the totality of the human person and thus avoid the fragmentation of society.

It is in the context of culture that the work of the investor is important. In attempting to account for the cultural diversity that characterizes the population, the investor does not operate in a universe of abstractions and illusions based on ideological prejudice. He or she rather remains firmly planted in reality, in our society as it is in its totality. One segment of our culturally diverse population, the developing Hispanic American culture, is a good case in point.

It is important to underline that this is a developing culture unique to the United States. It is being born as the result of an encounter, often dramatic, between the dominant North American culture and the culture born out of another multi-cultural encounter—namely, the encounter between the Iberian culture of the sixteenth century, African cultures, and those of the natives of the southern sector of the American hemisphere. The Hispanic-American culture being born of this encounter between the north and the south of the hemisphere will certainly be different from the Hispanic culture in the U.S. that existed prior to that encounter.

I believe that all attempts to create a cultural synthesis by means of ideological presuppositions are misguided and, in any case, sooner or later they will fail. It is not a question of "Americanizing" our Hispanic population, and certainly not of imposing Hispanic cultural prejudices on the rest of the American population. Nor is it a matter of creating a vast cultural ghetto within this country. It is a matter of an enrichment of both cultures born from the experience of encounter at the deepest level of human life, at the level of—yes, let us use the word—the level of the religious sense as described above. This is the level at which true cultural encounters occur and a new cultural synthesis is created.

Both the Hispanic and the Anglo-American cultures find their ultimate roots at this level. Their deepest differences originate in the dramatic split within Western Christianity called the Protestant Reformation, which occurred at the very dawn of the modern era, at the beginning of the European expansion into the New World. Latin America and Anglo-Saxon America are two different versions of this European expansion and the cultural synthesis born from it.

In Latin America, the deepest root of cultural unity became the religious sensitivity produced by the Baroque Catholicism of the sixteenth century. It is important to insist that I am not talking about the personal faith of the people living within this cultural unity. In fact, the concrete faith of the people varies. It includes Catholics, Protestants, Jews, syncretists, agnostics, and atheists. I am talking about religious sensibility, about that religious sense shaped by the experience of the insatiable demands of the heart. This sensibility suggests an attitude towards life, towards all aspects of life, including the life of faith.

I have summarized this attitude towards life in terms of three priorities: the priority of events over ideas, the priority of sign over appearance, and the priority of experience over feelings. The key point uniting these three is the fact that faith (and therefore hope, and therefore risk) is not detached from the experience of the meaning of life discovered through the religious sense.

In the United States, the underlying religious sensibility is completely different. Because of our nation's origins within the Protestant sectors of European expansion, best represented in the Calvinist religious atmosphere of the first settlers, faith and the experience of the desires of the human heart tend to be separated. These desires are suspected of being corrupted by sinful pride. This brings about a different basis for risk and for investment, a different view of work. The importance of work is experienced more as a matter of duty than desire, of responsibility more than adventure.

When these sensibilities come together, as they are doing now in the United States, their encounter need not betoken a divisive clash. Both represent different ways of interpreting the desires of the heart that are absolutely the same for all human beings. This experience, unimpeded by prejudices and pre-conditions, unencumbered by ideology, is the basis for a fruitful, creative dialogue that will benefit all sides of this encounter. It is a matter of creating an alliance with the heart of humankind by rejecting all ideological restrictions and emphasizing the sheer human greatness of creative risk-taking. It is a matter of expanding perspectives, and this happens the deeper we go into the attractions that motivate human freedom by embodying our orientation to infinity.

In the Flesh

The Family as Community

EVANGELIZATION IS THE proclamation of the *evangelion*, the gospel of Jesus Christ. This includes the proclamation of the gospel to those who have never heard it or to those for whom it has ceased to be a lived experience. The latter may be baptized Christians who no longer practice their faith, but it also includes those baptized Christians for whom faith is no longer a basis for judgments about what is true or false, right or wrong, desirable or undesirable. It is this latter context above all that gives rise to the call for a "new" evangelization. The New Evangelization presupposes that for many Catholics, the gospel is no longer experienced as a cultural proposal, a proposal for life in this world.

The term was first introduced by Pope John Paul II in his address to the bishops of Latin America on March 9, 1979, in Port-au-Prince, Haiti. He said that the present moment requires an evangelization that is new in "ardor, expression, and methods."

John Paul II was building on the process of renewal carried out by the Church in Latin America after the Second Vatican Council. Crucial to this effort was the relation between the gospel and culture. This has been a central consideration in all the great documents that have guided the work of the Church in Latin America, especially the Declarations of Medellín, Puebla, and Santo Domingo.

Among the signs of the times, the Second Vatican Council recognized the powerful attraction of an atheist humanism that excludes all considerations of transcendence, spirituality, and divinity from the quest for human fulfillment. The rationale behind this practical atheism is that such concerns are alienating, that is, they prevent human beings from seizing control of their own destiny. It was claimed that, by postponing human liberation to an after-life in heaven that was reached only by accepting the suffering of injustice on the earth, the Christian faith inculcated in people a sense of guilt and a resignation that played into the hands of the powerful. The dehumanizing poverty of so many in the Catholic countries of Latin America was seen as proof of the alienating nature of a faith that promised liberation only in a world beyond death.

The Council recognized that the gospel could not be credibly proposed as liberating unless it was clearly seen to compel believers to struggle for human liberation in this world. At its final session, Pope Paul VI said the Church was prepared to demonstrate that its humanism valued the human person more than atheist humanism did. Inspired by this conciliar teaching, the Church in Latin America began to explore the link between the gospel and the quest for social justice and liberation.

What came to be called "liberation theology" sought to relate the gospel to concrete social, political, and economic proposals. Based on the socio-economic Dependency Theory, liberation theology interpreted the gospel from the perspective of those who were engaged in revolutionary activity aimed at replacing the "structures of dependence" that held the nations of Latin America captive. The abandonment of Dependency Theory by social analysts and the crisis in Marxist thought following the collapse of communist states weakened significantly the influence of liberation theology. Yet, while criticizing its presuppositions, methodology, and conclusions, the Roman Magisterium could not ignore the questions it raised about the relation between the kingdom proclaimed by the gospel and the fate of individuals, peoples, and nations in this world. The New Evangelization must be understood as the response to these questions.

The New Evangelization signals an effort to retrieve the experience of the gospel as a stand with respect to life in this world—that is, as a cultural proposal. The gospel of Jesus Christ must be shown to be a way of life that leads men and women to encounter their destiny in this life. There is no authentic New Evangelization if this cultural dimension is neglected. Unless the New Evangelization takes seriously the present split between the gospel and culture, it will be seen as a retreat into individualistic piety.

Of course, evangelization cannot be reduced to the construction of a better world through social and political action. The kingdom of God does not belong to this world. Evangelization brings about a new creation which is the fruit of God's grace, not of human efforts. No amount of earthly progress will lead to the future which God's loving mercy has in store for us.

Still, the gospel is not the announcement of a purely otherworldly future. Evangelization is the announcement of an event, a fact: *et Verbum caro factum est*. The Word has become factual in the flesh, has become a fact, a presence in this world. If this presence, this fact, is not discernible to the senses, to the flesh, then the proclamation of the gospel will remain abstract and theoretical.

Evangelization is the announcement of an event that has taken place in this world, not only in the past, but through evangelization itself. Recall Saint Paul's "Now is the day of salvation" (2 Cor 6:2) and Christ's own "this Scripture passage is fulfilled in your hearing" (Lk 4:21). Evangelization makes the "event" happen in the present of the announcement.

What is the event that is made a present fact through evangelization?

It is not the triumph of an idea or system of values. The gospel is the person of Jesus Christ, and Jesus Christ is not an idea, but a concrete, specific, historical individual: the son of Mary—this child, this young man, this Jew who lived in a specific place and time. He is the savior, the redeemer, the destiny of human beings, individually and collectively. Evangelization makes present the fact of Jesus Christ, the power of his presence as the crucified and risen Lord, center of history and the cosmos.

The evangelists are those who give witness to what has happened to them when the power of the presence of the crucified and risen Lord took over their flesh—that is, their human life in this world. The evangelist is compelled to share this experience with others. Thus a "network of relations in the flesh" is created in this world: flesh-to-flesh in all directions of space and time. As such, the gospel always generates in this world bonds of friendship, companionship, solidarity, mutual presence, and inter-personal communion, bonds that cannot be destroyed by any power of this world.

Therefore, the life of faith in Christ betokens a new way of living in this world. It betokens the creation of an interpersonal communion called the Church, which is right in the middle of this world but whose origin and destiny lie beyond it. The life of the Church is the anticipation of the eschatological life of the kingdom expressed concretely, publicly, and visibly in terms of new relationships that the believer experiences with creation, with others, and with God.

We need a New Evangelization because for too many the experience of faith in Christ as a cultural proposal has been lost. For too many the life of the Church serves primarily as the way to satisfy spiritual needs. Or else the Church is seen as the promoter and custodian of key moral values that society needs. The latter is especially true in a time of social disintegration such as ours. It is a great temptation for the Church to reduce its mission to that of an ethical authority in order to gain access to the public forum. For this reason, the New Evangelization must make clear that the gospel of Jesus Christ is not the gospel of salvation through ethics; it is the gospel of salvation through a personal communion with Jesus Christ. He, and he alone, is the savior of the human race.

Instead, so often today the eternal life proclaimed to us by the gospel as the fruit of faith in Christ is little more than a beautiful idea offering us inspiration and promising a future consolation. Its value for this life resides solely in the interior peace it is said to give. Life in this world is thus abandoned to other factors, guided by considerations that have nothing to do with redemption by Christ experienced in the life of the Church. To be a Christian is too often reduced to the acceptance of a series of ideas and values, of concepts and traditions that remain unconvincing when separated from the experience of redemption in Christ. Thus, the personal and public moral life of so many Catholics is determined by compromises and calculations seeking to reconcile these "values" that have been detached from the experience of a personal relationship with Jesus Christ. Perceptions of value, judgments, and actions no longer flow from a lived experience of a surprising encounter with salvation and mercy. When this happens, the Christian faith ceases to be truly creative of different forms of social life. This is what has happened to too many Catholics, and this is one of the central concerns of the New Evangelization.

The New Evangelization therefore calls us to a retrieval of the foundational Christian experience of the person of Jesus Christ as the incarnate destiny of each human being. This includes the retrieval of the experience of the Church as the interpersonal communion where Jesus Christ is encountered today. The modern technological, functional mentality has created a world of replaceable individuals incapable of interpersonal communion. Society is grouped by artificial arrangements created by powerful interests. The New Evangelization must therefore create "ecclesial spaces" of life as alternative ways of life in this modern world. And this does not happen through ideas and concepts and programs. It happens when someone whose humanity is "cultivated" by the incarnate Son of God embraces without reservation someone who has not yet had this encounter, and they begin to experience a new way of being human together.

Nowhere is the modern age's radical inability to create or even understand how human beings are to live together clearer than in its inability to promote and sustain the family, the fundamental community of human life. We are facing efforts to radically re-define the family to make it fit the impoverished anthropology characteristic of modernity. In the most recent generations of Catholics, we are seeing a tragic loss of the experience of authentic family life. That is why the bishops of Latin America and the Caribbean, echoing the pastoral agenda of Pope John Paul II, called the family the "frontier" of the New Evangelization.

How is the evangelization of the family to proceed?

All families originate in the union between a man and a woman called marriage. Marriage is a union in the flesh; it is an event in the flesh of the man and the woman. According to divine revelation, the union in the flesh between a man and a woman is inseparable, in a mysterious way (a mega-mystery, Saint Paul calls it), from the union between Jesus Christ and humanity in the flesh. I suggest to you that the reason many Catholics have lost the experience of marriage and family is because they have lost the experience of the union between Jesus Christ and the human flesh of the Church. They have lost the sensibility of this ineffable union. They have allowed Jesus Christ to become dis-incarnate from human flesh, from their own flesh. Jesus Christ has become a remote figure, someone to be admired, even imitated (as much as possible), the name given to a memory that was once very powerful, but which every day dissipates more and more and no longer has the power to be the center of one's life. Jesus Christ is no longer experienced as a powerful, factual presence which has taken possession of our flesh to empower it to reach its destiny.

This is precisely what the New Evangelization aims to correct, to reverse, by a retrieval of the fundamental experiences characteristic of the following of Jesus Christ, experiences of the flesh and in the flesh. Without these, the renewal of marriage and family life is impossible, and the teaching of the Church will always remain external to real life. Detached from the event, the *factum* of the Incarnation, the teachings of the Church concerning marriage and family become utopian or plainly moralistic and legalistic. The evangelization of the family requires a retrieval of the experience of Christ as one who comes in the flesh.

According to Saint John, what distinguishes the spirits that come from God is their affirmation of Christ as the one who comes in the flesh. The separation of Christ from the flesh is the work of the Anti-Christ, the one with the power of the world at his disposal, the "prince of this world."

The evangelization of the family therefore requires the decision to confront this power when necessary: the power of the world, incarnate in the state, the media of social communications, and the great financial interests that set the pace of contemporary culture. The "family politics" to which John Paul II called us in his Apostolic Letter *Familiaris Consortio* must be above all a politics of resistance to these powers. But this must be a resistance originating not in alternative political theories or movements—that was the error of liberation theology—but in the experience of the presence, the fact of the presence of Jesus Christ in the flesh, the experience of the life of the Church.

There is no other way.

The Prophet is Always Someone Sent

Youth, Desire, and the Truth of the Heart

IN THE BROADWAY MUSICAL *West Side Story* there is a scene in which the owner of a soda-fountain typical of the 1950s is scandalized by the anger shown by a young member of a street gang after the killing of their leader by the head of another gang. The owner begins to tell the young man, "When I was your age. . . ." But the gang member interrupts him: "Get this thing clear, Doc. You was never my age!"

When I first saw the play back in the dinosaur age, when I was a young man just out of high school, I loved the young man's reply. It expressed so well what I wanted to say to all the elders who criticized my likes and dislikes, my vocabulary, my ideas, or any other aspect of my lifestyle that shocked them because they were not like that "when they were my age." The world had changed, I thought, and I had to live my life in circumstances that were very different from those of the time of their youth. I could not be expected to live by standards and ideas that were, as far as I could tell, outmoded. I had to be faithful to life as I knew it, not to life in the past.

I think about this each time I am asked to speak to young people. What do I know about how young people today experience the pressures and demands of life? Add to the age difference the fact that I lived the first seventeen years of my life in a cultural setting quite different from this one, in Puerto Rico. Consider also our differences in regional, social, economic, racial, and ethnic backgrounds. How could I ever imagine that I have anything to say to young people, no matter how hip, open, and cutting-edge I may consider myself? It is so true that, in this sense, I was never their age.

Yet I believe that no matter our differences, all human beings do have something in common—indeed, the most important thing. We have in common that we are human beings, human persons—and this is important. Some say that human persons are so different, that changes in lifestyles are so radical and histories, traditions, and backgrounds so unique, that there can be no real communication across those barriers. That is simply not so. What make us all human are those desires within ourselves that are exactly the same for all of us. We can call these the "original desires of the human heart"—original in the sense that they arise out of our origins, our very identity. These desires or exigencies or demands are what move us as human beings, move us to respond to reality as it impacts us, move us to look for the meaning of life, for its purpose, for whatever can make sense of the fact that we had no part in our own coming into being and now find ourselves existing in a world we did not create. Those desires are the same for all of us: the desire for peace, for freedom, for justice, for acceptance, for truth, for happiness—indeed for life itself.

All living things show something like these desires. All living things do what they have to do to keep living. I am a late-night person and love to watch documentaries about life in the wild, like those shown by the Discovery Channel or National Geographic. I even watch Animal Planet, and God knows how many times I have watched shows about crocodiles and sharks.

Actually, I am never really sure whether I have not already seen the show I'm looking at, because they are almost all the same. The plot is simple. It consists of four parts: hunt, eat, reproduce, and be eaten. It's amazing and terribly frustrating. These animals do not have a moment of peace. You can see it in their faces. They always look worried (except the very little ones who are relaxed because they do not know what's coming), even when they are reproducing, even when they are eating. They are looking behind their backs because any moment they might themselves become food or another of their own might move in fast and spirit away the prey that they spent one hundred hours racing to catch. It's amazing that they have any appetite.

Have you seen how terribly nervous birds are when they are eating? No wonder there are bird droppings all over afterwards. And yet on and on it goes. Life keeps trying to hang in there. It is only at the end, when hanging from the mouth of a tiger, that the zebras or the deer actually look serene and resigned. I tell you, if only one of them would change their tactics, like refuse to run, or stop suddenly and growl at their attacker, or jump into the water for the first time in their lives, the attacker might be so stunned and surprised that they could have a chance to make it. But no, that doesn't happen. These animals don't ever try anything really new.

And here's the difference between animals and human beings. Human beings look for and try out new things and tactics to sustain and enrich their lives. Human beings create what is new. And the most remarkable difference is that human beings hope to survive death itself. All life seeks to survive as long as possible; human life seeks eternity.

But how can this be? Where does the hope in human beings that death can be survived come from?

If the desires of the heart are the energy that moves us to action, what guides our life, our search for life, then, is that, in the case of human beings, these desires aim at infinity. They know no limit. Nothing will satisfy human desires except infinite life, infinite happiness, infinite peace and justice and beauty and truth.

This is why the desires of the human heart are different from survival instincts. Survival is not enough for us. Our hearts will be restless until they find the infinity for which they were made. And this is what brings us together across the divides of age, culture, race, country, and everything else that could make communication impossible were it not for these common desires and the infinity they seek.

What I want to say to you comes from the desires of my heart that are the same as those within each one of you. At this level, before the infinity that our hearts seek, we are the same age now.

In their search for infinity, human beings follow a path that we could call the religious sense. But we can see that people follow many different religions and that these depend on many factors that differ among humans, such as age, traditions, culture, temperament, philosophical and scientific convictions, and so forth. That is why there are a variety of religions in the world. Who can say whether one religion is better than another? As the expression of the different ways to search for what the heart seeks, they are something very personal and very intimate, and we should not expect them to be exactly the same (even though they have much in common). People are looking for infinity, and who can grasp the infinite, who can describe the mystery of infinity?

There is a Buddhist parable in which a king brings together ten of the wisest persons in the kingdom to show them an elephant. The problem is that these ten wise persons are blind, so they have not seen what an elephant is like. So, when the elephant is brought in, each one is allowed to touch it in order to form a mental image of it. And after all have touched the elephant, the king asks each to describe it. You can imagine what happens. Each one describes a different picture, depending on what they could touch with their hands. They have all touched the elephant, but they cannot grasp it in its totality. Each little part was right as it goes, each of the wise persons had indeed touched the same elephant, but the descriptions they gave of it could not be brought together to describe what an elephant is really like. Each account was true as far as it went, but none of them came even close to the truth of an elephant.

I think you can tell the point of the parable. The point of the parable is that God, because he is infinite, can never be grasped by any one religion. They may be on to something, recognize some aspect of God and infinity, but they cannot grasp the reality itself. Buddhists insist that anything we say about God distorts the reality because it reduces the deity to our level of vision (or blindness). No words can describe him; no desires can point to what God is like. Indeed, the best thing to do, the best religious path to follow, is to get rid of all these desires, even the desire for personal survival, even the desire to be yourself. Our destiny, at least from what it looks like to us, is Absolute Nothingness.

Now that has a nice, sophisticated, classy touch to it. Today many people are attracted by Buddhism because they are afraid of the violence and suffering and death that religions have caused under the pretense of being the one true religion that possesses the true knowledge of God, of infinity, of the mystery, and therefore of what our hearts seek. In the name of that truth, these religions tell you what your heart must seek or not seek. In order to follow them, you suppress some of those desires, or even all of them. You consider them irrational, infantile, illusory.

I can never be a Buddhist because I care too much about the desires in my heart. They are there no matter what I think, and, frankly, Absolute Nothingness sounds absolutely awful to me. Maybe it's because I'm presently fat. I have never seen fat Buddhist mystics. But even when I was very thin, I wanted many things because somehow they satisfied, even if partially, the desires of my heart. The infinity that I desire is not absolute nothing. If anything, it is absolute everything! And as far as the parable goes, all it tells me is that the infinity that my heart seeks is not an elephant.

Still, we must recognize that what is limited cannot grasp the totality of what is infinite, and that is why in the end all religions are really frustrating. That is why many people give up and settle for what is less than infinite, suppressing their desire for infinity.

And so this is the first piece of advice I offer: do not permit any power on earth to diminish or suppress the desires of your hearts for infinity. Those desires are real; they are part of being human. We cannot let anyone convince us or force us to be less than human. Being truly human is the condition for everything else. Nothing more can be expected of us than being human as intensely as possible.

The time of our youth, more than any other time, is the time for searching, for a passion for all that life has to offer us, for imagination and creativity. That is why young people pose the greatest threat to those who want to diminish or suppress the desires of the human heart. But why would anyone want to do that? They want to do that to keep us under their control. They want us to turn to them for our desires and needs, so that they can have power over us. They do this above all through the means of social communications at the service of powerful economic and advertising interests.

Their efforts have been overwhelmingly successful among young people. Today most young people look the same, dress the same, listen to the same music, celebrate the same personalities, share the same prejudices, all over the world. All over the world there is one dominant youth culture, which means that the dominant power has succeeded in lulling the desires of the hearts of the young for infinity. And the moment we lose our link with infinity, we lose our freedom, and we fall into the hands of the powerful who have no mercy.

Youth ministry must seek to set young people free from this manipulation that has made so many of them so boringly the same, like airports that look the same no matter where you are or like most suburban Chinese restaurants at lunch time, offering the same menu wherever you are, from New York to Long Beach, California. Have you noticed that if you go late at night to these places you see Chinese natives eating all kinds of strange exotic things that are not on the menu?

That is what we must be like in the great Chinese restaurant of life. We must show that we have not succumbed to the sameness imposed by the ruling economic, cultural, social, or political powers, that the link between the desires of our heart and infinity have not been weakened or even severed.

What do we call that which rescues us from this manipulation? What do we call that which sets us free by affirming our link with the infinite mystery that lies at the origin and destiny of our lives, the mystery who put its mark on us by creating us with desires for its infinity in our hearts? It's called the truth. It is the truth that sets us free. Everything else is a lie; it is deception. And it is deception that enslaves us, diminishes us, and manipulates us.

A prophet is the one who tells us the truth. Madame Cleo of late-night TV claims to be able to do that by reading Tarot cards. In the Bronx where I live, many Madame Cleos open up chickens to discover what the future holds, and in the nicest buildings in Manhattan they read their horoscopes. But a prophet is not the one who tells us what will happen in the future. The prophet tells us the truth about the desires of our heart. The prophet tells us what our heart really desires when we feel desires that confuse us or even mislead us. And the prophet tells us that what our hearts desire is the infinite mystery that created us and that is our destiny. The prophet speaks words and performs gestures that put us in direct contact with that mystery. For this reason, the prophet is always someone sent, because no one can reach that mystery by his or her own powers—as indeed the religious sense shows us if we pursue it without giving up, without stopping along the way and declaring the mystery to be contained by what we have found.

Whatever takes the place of the mystery is an idol, and the prophet is the opponent of idols, unmasking them as false, as not truth. Idols need not be statues of lizards or strange-looking creatures. An idol is anything that pretends to be the infinite mystery that our heart seeks. Political parties can be idols; countries can be idols; philosophical systems like communism, fascism, socialism, or capitalism can be idols. Democracy, the state, or the market, religious groups, race and ethnic origin, money and sex—all of these can be idols if they are identified with the infinite mystery that your heart seeks.

The prophet opposes all these idols, which tells you why prophets are frequently killed.

Jesus Christ is a prophet. But more than just a prophet. He is *the* prophet, the only prophet there is. All other authentic prophets were chosen men and women who anticipated him, who saw him from afar, as he said himself, and rejoiced. Such was the case of the prophets of Israel who prepared his way and even now care for the destiny of the people to which they were sent. That is why it was so important for the evangelists and the apostles to show that all prophesies were fulfilled in him and by him.

He is the prophet of prophets because he alone unveils the full truth about what it means to be a human being. He alone knows, and cares for fully, everything that makes us human. The human person is a mystery, and all purely human knowledge is as blind to the full truth about man and woman as the ten wise persons of the Buddhist parable trying to figure out what an elephant is. Sociology cannot exhaust the truth about the human person. Psychiatry cannot do it. Biology cannot do it. Genetics cannot do it. Philosophies cannot do it. Economics cannot do it. They may grasp bits and pieces here and there, but the only one who unveils man to man himself is Jesus Christ the Prophet.

Jesus Christ unveils the truth because he is the truth, as he is the way and the life, the origin by whom and for whom all that exists was created, the past who rescues and preserves forever all human loves, all human creative initiatives, all human hopes, preserving all from corruption and death. He is the present giving meaning, value, sense, and depth to all authentic human efforts to discover the truth about the infinity for which we were created. And he is the future, our infinite destiny itself, since it was to share his life in his Body that we were created. His is the life that our hearts desire; it is because of him that all human life seeks eternity. Jesus Christ is the eternity all life seeks. He doesn't tell us about the infinite mystery. He *is* that infinite mystery in human flesh, his face the human face of the mystery, his gestures the human gestures of the mystery, his eyes the human eyes of the mystery, his words the human words of the mystery.

He is the prophet who knows what is in the human heart, as the evangelist says. Remember his meeting with the Samaritan woman at the well. Remember when he told her that she had no husband, that she had gone through five husbands and the man with whom she was living was not her husband. What did she say to him? What did she call him? She said, "Sir, I can see that you are a prophet" (Jn 4:19). And when she got back home so excited because she had met him, what did she say to the Samaritans? She said that she had met a man who had "told her everything she had done" (Jn 4:29).

Pay attention to her words. He had told her everything, not just about her love life, but everything about herself. He knew what was in her heart. He knew the desires of her heart for infinity, and he revealed them to her. That was her experience in encountering Jesus Christ. She found someone who knew her perfectly, who allowed her to know herself, who accepted and affirmed fully her humanity, whose companionship, presence, and words corresponded perfectly, like nothing else ever had, with the desires of her heart.

From that moment everything that satisfied her desires had to go through him, so to speak, had to correspond to her experience of being with him, of being united with him, of belonging to him. Or else it was not really what her heart desired; it was not really what she was made for, what would make her happy forever, what would set her free forever. Now the mystery was not just some infinity, desired but impossible to reach. Now the mystery had a face and a name: Jesus Christ. This is exactly what Paul repeats again and again: for him, life is Christ; his true life now is hidden with Christ in God, its goodness, its meaning, its value, and its sense assured and preserved by Christ; it was Christ who lived in him and through him, it was Christ for whom the universe was created. Thus Christ is the truth of creation, the truth of all that exists as it came from the hands of the infinite mystery; that is why Jesus Christ is all in all.

This is the experience of all who have encountered Jesus Christ and know him to be the prophet. This is my experience, too, and it is why I do not hesitate to address my words to youth. We can say equally: this is what moves my heart and my life, what sustains my hopes and corresponds to the desires of my heart: not a bunch of ideas or values or possessions or a philosophy of life or a political commitment, but a concrete person. We are not saved by ideas, Pope John Paul told the world's youth, we are saved by a person, by Jesus Christ.

But whoever follows Christ shares in his mission. Through our baptism into him we share his prophetic mission as we share his priestly and royal missions. We are anointed by the Spirit to be prophets in him and with him.

In Pope John Paul II's writings, Jesus Christ shows himself to be the prophet when he stands innocent before Pilate who threatens him with his power and tells him that he has come to bear witness to the truth (recall how Pilate asks "what is truth?"). We are prophets, his prophets, when we do the same before the Pilates of this world who cynically use their power to threaten those who have not lost their sense of the truth about what it means to be a human person.

This means that we must always be witnesses and defenders of the true desires of the human heart and their orientation and capacity for infinity. We must be the defenders and protectors of all that is authentically human. We must be promoters of true freedom. We must be apostles of the incomparable and ineffable dignity of each human being without exception, from the moment of conception to the moment when Christ comes to preserve that dignity forever. We must be witnesses to the truth of what it means to be a man or a woman, a father or mother, a husband or wife, a worker, a citizen of this country and this world, an artist, a scientist, a health practitioner, or whatever our heart calls us to be in whatever circumstances we find ourselves. That is why we must not allow anyone to tell us that our desires and hope for eternity, for justice, for peace, for freedom, for faithful and permanent friendship and companionship are illusions or vain dreams. Without Christ they would be. But we have Christ the Prophet, and we are his prophets.

Here's a story I like to tell. Luigi Giussani once ran into a young couple that were making out on a romantic, starry night. You can imagine how astounded they were at suddenly seeing this guy wearing a cassock standing there during such an intimate moment. Giussani smiled and said hello. "Tell me one thing," he said. "What you are doing now, how is it related to the stars?" Of course they were speechless, and probably relieved to think that the intruder was a bit mad.

Do you understand his question?

The stars stand for the infinity that all human hearts desire. This image is central to a poem written by the Spanish poet Federico Garcia Lorca, for whom stars play a very important symbolic role. He wrote a poem about an old snail who runs into a pack of red ants who are beating up on a young ant, and he asks them what is going on. They tell him that the young ant had hurt their highly organized work technique by climbing up a tree and getting totally out of control because, for the first time ever, she had seen the stars shining in the sky. The ants, whose work assignment did not permit them to climb trees, had never seen stars. They had never looked up. They did not know what the stars were. And neither did the snail!

So he asks the young ant, who tries to explain, even though she had been mortally wounded, "What are the stars?" The young ant tries to describe them as the eyes of the heavens, but he has no idea what she is talking about. The other ants get even more upset and violent. Eventually the young wounded ant dies, and the others leave to continue their work. No doubt there would be a replacement for the dead ant.

The snail stays there for a little while, wondering about the meaning of what had happened, wondering about the stars. In the distance he hears a bell announcing that dawn is coming. People are getting up to go to church. For a brief moment, the snail wonders if he too could climb a tree and see the stars. But in the end he doesn't, because he thinks that he is too clumsy, too heavy to climb up a tree. So he goes on along through the forest, thinking about his uncertainties, until one day he forgets the strange incident of the young ant and the stars.

The stars in the poem and in Giussani's question stand for the infinite destiny for which we are made. We are made of the thirst and hunger for this infinity, for this mystery. That is what makes us human. Freedom is the capacity to reach this infinite destiny and thus satisfy the desires of the heart. Isn't it when you are satisfied that you feel the most free? If you are not satisfied, if you cannot find and have what your heart desires, do you still feel free, even if no one is forcing you to do anything? Such freedom is totally meaningless, useless. The freedom we appreciate is the one that allows us to find and enjoy what satisfies our hearts.

This is why when our link with infinity is cut off, we are no longer free. We are like the ants that had not seen the stars. We may be great workers. We might be socially productive and accomplish all sorts of useful things that bring us food and protection from adversity, but we are not free. Each truly free human act—each truly human act, I should say, because if it is not free it is not human—links us with infinity, with the stars. Otherwise it will never satisfy the desires of the human heart.

That is why Giussani asked the question of those young lovers. How was the love they were expressing to each other related to the stars? How were their gestures related to the love that is linked to the stars? We must ask this of all that we do. Otherwise it is not worthy of us. This is the basis for a true morality. Our one moral obligation is to be fully human, that is, created for infinity.

To be a prophet is to give witness to the truth that each truly human act, each act of human freedom, is linked to our infinite destiny. Otherwise, it is not worthy of us. We must give this witness, we must proclaim this truth in all areas of human activity: human love, human work, human leisure, human politics, human economic strategies, human relations and friendships. In all of these areas we must remind this society and this culture that without our relation to the stars, human life makes no sense. This is what it means to stand prophetically with Christ before this society, this culture, this world. And for this we must be willing to be persecuted by the Pilates of this world who have never seen the stars or have totally forgotten them. We must be willing to be martyrs, either by losing our actual earthly lives or by suffering the martyrdom of ridicule and social exile.

There are three areas in which young people are especially called to offer this prophetic witness.

The first area is economic power. Young people today have tremendous economic resources, and very big bucks are made by the powers that influence or control them to buy their music, articles of clothing, technological gadgets, cars—and even their soft drinks and burgers. These powers will do everything to manipulate desires, to create new desires, to substitute some desires for others in order to enslave the young and control them. We must find ways to refuse to go along with their tactics. We must refuse to be manipulated this way. We must ask the Giussani question of everything we want to acquire: how is it related to the stars? We must demand that those who would sell us something tell us how their products are related to the infinity for which the heart beats. We must demand that they tell us how their economic strategies affect the poor, whose dignity, whose link with infinity is being violated by not being able to afford their basic needs, who have been refused the chance to express their creativity through dignified work and become instead resigned to being eaten up by beasts more powerful than those on the Discovery Channel. Then we will be prophets with Christ the Prophet.

The second area is education. Youth is a privileged time for education. The true teacher is the prophet. Jesus Christ is also the Teacher.

To educate is to "lead-out," to help human beings direct their lives away from themselves towards all of reality, all the way to the stars. All educational systems closed to the stars are inhuman. This has nothing to do with separation between church and state, with any particular political proposal to keep out, or, for that matter, introduce specific religious creeds into the public schools. This has to do with what it means to be a human being and therefore what a fully human education is like. As such it is an education in freedom. An education that closes off our vision of the stars is nothing but training to play our part in society at the service of the most powerful.

The third area is friendship, companionship, community, shared life. In a way, the ease with which the dominant economic powers have been able to create such a homogeneous world of the young reveals their great desire for acceptance, for companionship, for friendship. And yet, the world they have created for our young people is a world of radical isolation and loneliness, as newspaper headlines reveal practically every day. This is because in order to increase their power over the young, they have blocked the stars from their view. It is the capacity for infinity that creates community, friendship, solidarity, companionship, because these are established by being together in the encounter with something greater, something infinite. Take away this greater, and the bonds of unity and friendship—so dependent on mercy and forgiveness—disappear, because individual identity disappears as well. And then it is no longer possible to say "I" or "you" or "us."

That is why Jesus Christ said that the only thing that would convince the world that he is the "one sent"—the prophet—is the unity, the shared life among his disciples, a unity that reveals his true identity in the mystery of the Father, Son, and Spirit. A true encounter with Jesus will always lead to shared life because he is the someone greater who creates communion. We cannot be fully human in isolation. In isolation we cannot be free. We become someone by belonging together to someone greater.

We come together because we have encountered Christ. Now we must stay together, or the encounter will disappear, and this experience will become a memory of what could have been, instead of a stunning awareness of what is. In the end, this is the only way to be prophets in Christ the Prophet.

Acknowledgments

We gratefully acknowledge the support of the Albacete Forum in the production of this book. We are similarly indebted to Crossroads Cultural Center.

Our thanks to Godspy.com for permission to reprint "Between Now and Eternity," originally published under the title "Faith, Politics and the Scandal of Christ."

Lisa thanks her children—Joan, Clare, Benedict, and Ignatius—for their willingness, day in and day out, to respect the closed door of her hermitage that she might complete her work.

Greg is grateful for the love and support he receives from his wife Suzanne, children Magdalen, Helena, Charles, and Benedict, and grandchildren Esther, Aya, and Penelope.

This book was set in Adobe OFL Sorts Mill Goudy, designed by Barry Schwartz and published by The League of Moveable Type, the first open-source font foundry. Based on the classic Goudy Oldstyle, this typeface retains the strong influence of calligraphy that characterized its predecessor.

This book was designed by Shannon Carter, Ian Creeger, and Gregory Wolfe. It was published in hardcover, paperback, and electronic formats by Wipf and Stock Publishers, Eugene, Oregon.

CPSIA information can be obtained
at www.ICGtesting.com
Printed in the USA
LVHW031359020221
678123LV00011BA/316/J